FINANCE
FOR NONFINANCIAL
MANAGERS

Finance for Small Business

Basic Finance Concepts

Finance for Non Finance Managers

Murugesan Ramaswamy

FINANCE FOR NONFINANCIAL MANAGERS
(Ed-2.1)

Copyright © 2015-2021 by Murugesan Ramaswamy

The author of this publication has made every reasonable attempt to provide the highest accuracy in the content of this book. However, he assumes no responsibility for errors or omissions. You should use this book as you deem fit and at your own risk. Likely, the examples may not apply in your situation, and you should adjust your use of the information accordingly.

How can you benefit from this book?

Finance for Nonfinancial Managers (FNFMS) is a Quick Reference Finance Handbook to learn to read and interpret Financial Statements and understand financial management core concepts.

The book explains complex concepts in an easy-to-understand simple language.

Results-oriented approach to learning not only the financial tools but also understand their limitations. The book highlights symptoms of financial bankruptcy and the basics of turnaround strategies.

Topics are around your quest for knowledge in managing the financial performance of your business.

You will learn to interpret financial statements and make business decisions with a financial focus. Kindly be aware that this book will not make you at par with qualified finance professionals. You will not compete with a finance person in his trade; in fact, the finance person will complement your strength.

Always consult finance professionals for decisions having long-term financial implications.

Budding finance professionals can benefit from select topics — MIS Reports, working capital management, budgeting, and break-even analysis.

Study Plan

Chapter 1: Understand the Basics

Chapters 2 to 4: Get To Know the Financial Statements

Chapters 5 to 7: Learn to Read and Interpret Financial Statements

Chapters 8 to 10: Planning and Control in Finance

Chapters 9 & 12: Capital Expenditure Budgeting & Borrowing

If something is not clear, you are welcome to write to me, and I would love to assist you.

What FNFMS is NOT

FNFMS is **NOT** for **share market investments** or **personal finance.**

About the Author

The author is a Chartered Accountant from India. He has over thirty years of Finance domain experience in Logistics, Manufacturing Engineering, Real Estate, and Infrastructure business verticals.

You can contact the author at murugesan0202@yahoo.com.

∞○∞

Table of Contents

CHAPTER 1

The Finance Basics

What you do today can improve all your tomorrows - Ralph Marston

∞

Our lives change. We need to prepare for the changes. Finance for Nonfinancial Managers book attempts to help you cope with the emerging scenarios where you need knowledge on Finance.

Scenario 1: You are a startup entrepreneur, and you want to learn finance.

Scenario 2: Your new job demands financial performance-focused decision-making.

Scenario 3: You want to learn finance and achieve greater heights on the corporate ladder.

Let us learn finance, so it is no more a complex subject.

Are you ready? Here we go.

Chapter Contents

1. Accounting Methods
2. Double Entry Book Keeping
3. Terms Often Used
4. Financial Statements, an Intro

∞

1. Accounting Methods

As a foundation to learning Finance, we need basic accounting knowledge.

We record the company's financial transactions applying one of the two accounting methods. Therefore, knowledge of those accounting methods is necessary for learning Finance.

The Accounting Methods are i) Cash Basis Accounting and ii) Accrual Basis Accounting.

i) Cash Basis Accounting

Cash basis accounting means accounting based on cash payments and receipts. In simple words, the cash basis accounting method records cash payments as the expense and cash receipts as income.

For example, rent paid to the landlord is accounted as rent expense. Similarly, the cash received from a customer is an income.

From the above definition and the examples, the cash basis accounting method appears to be the correct method.

However, the cash-basis accounting method suffers a severe drawback when accounting for the *timing difference* of the cash receipts and payments.

Consider an advance payment towards an expense, such as rent paid in advance. Applying the Cash Basis Accounting, accountants treat the advance paid as an expense and not an advance payment.

Thus, in the cash method of accounting, cash payments, including an advance, are expenses, and cash receipts, including an advance received, are income. Also, any unpaid expense or future obligation is not an expense. Similarly, sales against differed receipts are not income.

From the above narrations, we understand the deficiency of the Cash Basis Accounting. Cash basis accounting is not the correct accounting method because of inaccuracies in the net profit or loss computations.

ii) Accrual Basis Accounting

The accrual basis accounting is the accounting method that recognizes the timing difference between

- ✓ Income and receiving the money against that income, and
- ✓ Expense and paying money towards that expense.

An example will make this simple.

Consider, a company accounts sales for Jan 20XX as income. Then the company should account for Jan 20XX expenses in the same month to compute the net Profit.

Please note such expense may have been paid /to be paid /paid in advance.

Expenses **paid in the same month** include salaries & wages paid at the end of the month.

Expenses **paid in advance** include office & showroom rent paid for one year in advance.

Expenses payable **in the future** include staff bonuses.

We understand the accrual accounting methods. Next, let's learn double-entry book-keeping, the fundamental concept of the accrual accounting method.

2. Double Entry Book Keeping

You may give a quick glance over this topic, and no need for an in-depth understanding.

The double-entry system of book-keeping is the fundamental accounting concept. This concept recognizes that every financial transaction has two effects.

Let us look at few examples to make it simple.

Examples 1: Company buys machinery from cash on hand:

> Accounting effect 1: *Increase in Assets,* machinery.
> Accounting effect 2: *Decrease in another asset,* cash.

Example 2: The company buys a car by arranging a loan with a bank.

Accounting effect 1: *Increase in Assets,* machinery.
Accounting effect 2: *Increase in liability,* bank loan.

Example 3: The company buys machinery, paid by the owners to start the business.

Accounting effect 1: *Increase in Assets,* machinery.
Accounting effect 2: Increase in equity, capital account.

Both effects of a financial transaction are entered in the accounting system as debit and credit.

Accounting entry for example 1:

Debit: Machinery A/c (asset a/c)
Credit: Cash A/c

Accounting entry for example 2:

Debit: Machinery A/c
Credit: Loan A/c (liability a/c)

Accounting entry for example 3:

Debit: Machinery A/c
Credit: Capital A/c (equity)

Thus, the two effects of every financial transaction are entered in the accounting system as a double entry, debit, and credit.

Now, let's get familiar with some of the often used terms in Finance.

∞

3. Terms Often Used

i) Fund, Money, and Cash

The terms fund, money, and cash are used in this book synonymously. But there is a subtle difference; cash denotes currency notes and coins while the term fund is used in a broader meaning to include other forms of cash such as dues from a customer. While we use the term money in a non-commercial language, for example, 'you lend money to your friend,' the term fund is often used in commercial transactions such as 'funding the working capital.'

ii) Sales, Revenue, And Turnover

Sales, revenue, and turnover are used synonymously to mean the company's earnings.

iii) Inventory and Stock

Inventory and stock refer synonymously to raw materials, work-in-progress, finished goods, and consumables.

iv) Borrowing and Debt

Borrowing and debt mean synonymously to loans to run the business.

v) Activity Level

Activity level refers to:

> Capacity utilization for a production facility;
> The sales quantity or sales amount for a trading company; and
> Quantum of service for a company such as a firm of lawyers.

As an illustration, consider a company's production unit is operating at 80% of its capacity. So, 80% is the activity level.

Activity level measures are helpful in budgeting and break-even analysis.

We understand the essential accounting methods and terms used in Finance.

Let's learn now about Financial Statements.

4. Financial Statements, an Intro

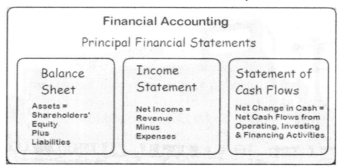

Financial statements are reports from financial accounting comprising Balance Sheet, Profit & Loss Account, and Cash Flow Statement.

Standard formats of Financial Statements have two years' values, the *Current Year* and the *Previous Year*.

i) Current Year

The current year is the year for which the financial statements are prepared and reviewed.

The current year may coincide with the calendar year—1 Jan to 31 Dec or any twelve months depending on the legal requirements.

Examples: *1 Apr 2014 to 31 Mar 2015, 1 Jul 2014 to 30 Jun 2015.*

iv) The Previous Year

The previous year is the twelve months preceding the current year.

1 Jan 2013 to 31 Dec 2013 is the previous year in our models (Exhibit 2.2 marked B.)

Two-year values help make an apple-to-apple comparison of values.

∞

Next, in Chapters 2, 3 & 4, we will learn Balance Sheet, Profit and Loss Account, and Cash Flow Statement.

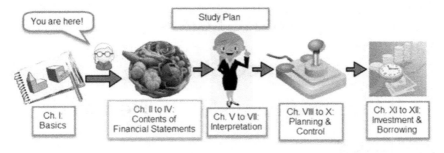

∞∞

CHAPTER 2

Balance Sheet —

the Financial Health Report

The Balance Sheet provides you with a complete picture of a company's financial health. It narrates owners' funds, debts, and assets.

Let's learn the Balance Sheet in this chapter.

Chapter Contents

1. The Balance Sheet Model
2. The Balance Sheet Date
3. Balance Sheet Concept
4. Assets
5. Owners' Equity
6. Liabilities
7. Significance of Current & Non-current Classification
8. Depreciation & Amortization

∞

1. The Balance Sheet Model

Exhibit 2.1 is the model Balance Sheet & Exhibit 2.2 breaks down the
Balance Sheet into its components.

Model Company Balance Sheet as at 31 Dec 2014			
Description	Line no.	2014 (Current year)	2013 (Previous year)
ASSETS			
Non-current assets			
Land		175,000	175,000
Property and equipment		451,255	429,006
Furniture & fixtures		44,938	45,000
Total non-current assets	(i)	671,193	649,006
Current assets			
Inventory		350,988	325,411
Trade and other receivables		401,855	310,879
Other current assets		12,819	11,470
Cash & bank		105,660	96,679
Total current assets	(ii)	871,322	744,439
Total assets	iii = (i+ii)	1,542,515	1,393,445
EQUITY & LIABILITIES			
Equity			
Capital		200,000	200,000
Reserves		100,000	100,000
Retained earnings		439,729	394,042
Total equity	(iv)	739,729	694,042
Non-current liabilities			
Long term debt		345,000	255,000
Total Non-current liabilities	(v)	345,000	255,000
Current liabilities			
Trade and other payables		196,850	198,527
Other current liabilities		50,936	50,876
Current portion of long term debt		210,000	195,000
Total current liabilities	(vi)	457,786	444,403
Total equity & liabilities	vii = (iv+v+vi)	1,542,515	1,393,445
Exhibit 2.1			

Model Company
Balance Sheet as at 31 Dec 2014   A

Description	Line no.	2014 (Current year)	2013 (Previous year)
ASSETS			
Non-current assets			
Land		175,000	175,000
Property and equipment		451,255	429,006
Furniture & fixtures		44,938	45,000
Total non-current assets	(i)	**671,193**	**649,006**
Current assets			
Inventory		350,988	325,411
Trade and other receivables		401,855	310,879
Other current assets		12,819	11,470
Cash & bank		105,660	96,679
Total current assets	(ii)	**871,322**	**744,439**
Total assets	iii = (i+ii)	**1,542,515**	**1,393,445**
EQUITY & LIABILITIES			
Equity			
Capital		200,000	200,000
Reserves		100,000	100,000
Retained earnings		439,729	394,042
Total equity	(iv)	**739,729**	**694,042**
Non-current liabilities			
Long term debt		345,000	255,000
Total Non-current liabilities	(v)	**345,000**	**255,000**
Current liabilities			
Trade and other payables		196,850	198,527
Other current liabilities		50,936	50,876
Current portion of long term debt		210,000	195,000
Total current liabilities	(vi)	**457,786**	**444,403**
Total equity & liabilities	vii = (iv+v+vi)	**1,542,515**	**1,393,445**

Assets = Equity + Liabilities

Exhibit 2.2

∞

10

2. The Balance Sheet Date

The Balance Sheet is on a *specific date*—31 Dec 2014 (Exhibit 2.2 marked A.) This is the *Balance Sheet date*.

So, what is the importance of the Balance Sheet date?

The Balance Sheet explains a company's assets, debts, and owners' funds on a particular date—the Balance Sheet date.

We know any financial item changes with time. Therefore, the date is significant in the study of a Balance Sheet.

Thus, a Balance Sheet is a list of a company's financial items as on a specific date.

∞

3. Balance Sheet Concept

A Balance Sheet is a balanced statement of *Equity and Liabilities* on one side and *Assets* and on the other side (Exhibit 2.2 marked C.).

$$Equity + Liabilities = Assets$$

The startup stage

Owners contribute the capital amount.

Applying the double-entry book-keeping concept we discussed in the last chapter,

> The company's bank account (asset) is debited
>
> Capital account (owners' equity) is credited.

The company borrows from the bank:

> Bank account (asset) is debited
>
> The loan account (liability) is credited.

Machinery purchase:

> Plant & Machinery account (asset) is debited
>
> Bank account (asset) is credited

Observing the above transactions, we understand, equity and liabilities are the funding transactions to acquire the assets.

That is, Equity + Liabilities = Assets

Thus, the total value of equity plus liabilities is equal to assets in the Balance Sheet.

Transactions to earn a profit

Now, what happens when the company spends money to earn an income? How does the equilibrium maintained between the equity plus liabilities on one side and the assets on the other side of the Balance Sheet?

A company, in its business activity, spends money to earn an income. It results in a profit or loss.

When the result is a profit—i) it increases assets, say cash, and ii) the profit is added to equity as it belongs to owners. When there is a loss, it is the opposite effect. Loss reduces assets, say cash, and there is a corresponding reduction in equity.

Thus, in a Balance Sheet, the sum of equity and liabilities is equal to the assets. This is the Balance Sheet concept; the total value of Equity plus Liabilities matches the total value of Assets.

∞

4. Assets

Let's now understand the Assets in a Balance Sheet.

Assets are the properties owned by the company. Assets include:

> Land,
> Plant & Machinery,
> Vehicles,
> Furniture & Fittings,
> Inventory,
> Customer balances against credit sales, and
> Cash & Bank balance.

We classify assets into i) non-current and ii) current assets.

The classification is based on the *assets' use* in the business, whether they are required for *running the business* or *acquired and turned over in the course of the company's business.*

If this sounds too complicated, don't worry. As we study the next two topics, you will understand the asset classification concept.

i) Non-current Assets

We classify assets such as Plant & Machinery and Vehicles **used for running the business** as non-current assets. *Please refer to D in the model Balance Sheet—Exhibit 2.2.*

The company acquires non-current assets to use them in the business; plant and machinery for production and vehicles for transportation.

Usually, non-current assets have a life span exceeding one year. Upon usage, they diminish in their value. End of their useful life, companies sell them as scrap.

The difference between the assets' purchase cost and their scrap value is charged as depreciation in accounting.

We will learn how the companies calculate and charge off depreciation later in this chapter.

ii) Current Assets

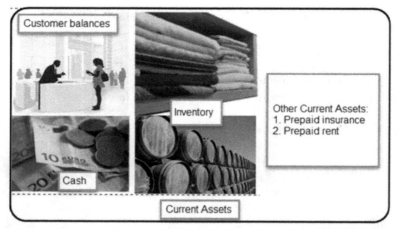

Current assets are those assets acquired and turned over **in the course of the business** (Exhibit 2.2, marked E.)

Examples of current assets:

- ✓ Materials purchased for production (raw material inventory) or sales (merchandise inventory);
- ✓ Customer dues (Receivables); and
- ✓ Cash balance.

Please note trucks purchased by a company for the delivery of goods are non-current assets. However, for a truck dealer, trucks in his showroom are current assets (inventory.)

In the Balance Sheet, **current assets** are classified and grouped as

   a) Inventory,

   b) Trade and other receivables,

   c) Other current assets, and

   d) Cash and Bank.

a) Inventory

Inventory includes

> Raw materials,
>
> Work-in-process,
>
> Finished goods, and
>
> Consumables.

b) Trade and Other Receivables

The term 'Trade Receivables' refers to dues from customers. Examples of other receivables include the amount due from the company's employees towards salary advance and staff loan.

c) Other Current Assets

Other current assets include expenses paid in advance. Example: rent and insurance paid for the future period.

d) Cash & Bank

'Cash & Bank' in the Balance Sheet refers to the cash balance held by the company to meet the daily cash expenses and cash balance in the company's bank account.

We have learned the Balance Sheet's Assets side. Next, we'll learn Equity & Liabilities side.

∞

5. Owners' Equity

Model Company
Balance Sheet as at 31 Dec 2014

Description	Line no.	2014 (Current year)	2013 (Previous year)
ASSETS			
Non-current assets			
Land		175,000	175,000
Property and equipment		451,255	429,006
Furniture & fixtures		44,938	45,000
Total non-current assets	(i)	**671,193**	**649,006**
Current assets			
Inventory		350,988	325,411
Trade and other receivables		401,855	310,879
Other current assets		12,819	11,470
Cash & bank		105,660	96,679
Total current assets	(ii)	**871,322**	**744,439**
Total assets	iii = (i+ii)	**1,542,515**	**1,393,445**
EQUITY & LIABILITIES			
Equity	Ⓕ		
Capital		200,000	200,000
Reserves		100,000	100,000
Retained earnings		439,729	394,042
Total equity	(iv)	**739,729**	**694,042**
Non-current liabilities	Ⓖ		
Long term debt		345,000	255,000
Total Non-current liabilities	(v)	**345,000**	**255,000**
Current liabilities	Ⓗ		
Trade and other payables		196,850	198,527
Other current liabilities		50,936	50,876
Current portion of long term debt		210,000	195,000
Total current liabilities	(vi)	**457,786**	**444,403**
Total equity & liabilities	vii = (iv+v+vi)	**1,542,515**	**1,393,445**

Exhibit 2.3

Owners' equity or simply equity is the owners' money. In the Balance Sheet, owners' equity is the sum of Capital, Reserves & Surplus, and Retained Earnings (Exhibit 2.3, F.)

i) Capital

Capital represents the core funding by the owners to start or expand the business.

For companies governed by corporate laws, capital is referred to as *equity capital* or *share capital;* in a partnership or a proprietorship, capital is *partners' or proprietor's capital.*

Characteristics of Capital

The capital in a business is

- ✓ Eligible for Profit,
- ✓ Not eligible for interest, and
- ✓ Restrictions apply for returning the capital to the owners.

Usually, for small businesses that are not governed by corporate laws, there may not be any restrictions to pay interest on the capital and return the capital to the owners.

iii) Reserves and Surplus

Reserves are part of the owners' equity. Reserves are available for distribution to the owners as:

- ✓ Dividend, and
- ✓ Bonus shares.

iv) Retained Earnings

The Profit that remains after paying the dividend is added to Retained Earnings Account.

The company can use the Retained Earnings account balance for:

- ✓ Distribution to owners as dividend, or
- ✓ Transfer to Reserves and Surplus Account.

∞

6. Liabilities

We will now discuss liabilities under the 'Equity & Liabilities' side of the Balance Sheet.

The amount owed by the company to an outsider is a liability. Liabilities arise because of i) borrowings and ii) the purchase of goods and services on credit.

Thus, liabilities include:

Money borrowed,

Suppliers' balances, and

Expenses payable.

Similar to assets classification, we classify liabilities into non-current and current liabilities.

Let's learn now what are non-current and current liabilities.

i) Non-current Liabilities

Non-current liabilities are debts or loans due for payment exceeding one year from the Balance Sheet date.

In the Balance Sheet model depicted, long-term debt (marked G) is a non-current liability.

ii) Current Liabilities

Liabilities payable in the *ordinary course of business* and debt or any portion of long-term debt payable within one year from the Balance Sheet date are current liabilities (Exhibit 2.3, H.)

Current liabilities include amounts due:

- ✓ To suppliers against the purchase of inventory,
- ✓ Towards expenses payable, and
- ✓ Against loans and bank borrowings, the repayable amount within one year from the Balance Sheet date.

∞

7. Significance of Current and Non-current Classification

We need the current and non-current classification of assets and liabilities to measure the company's financial liquidity. Liquidity refers to the ability of the company to pay off its immediate liabilities.

Liquidity is a factor of paramount importance for business continuity.

To measure liquidity, we need to know the amount of immediate financial commitments viz., current liabilities, and the means of meeting those commitments viz., current assets.

We will discuss more on liquidity under Chapter 7 Ratio Analysis (page 62.)

∞

8. Depreciation and Amortization

We know assets such as land, building, plant & machinery are non-current assets. We classify non-current assets into tangible and intangible assets.

Tangible assets are assets such as buildings, machinery, and vehicles. They are 'tangible,' meaning 'physical' assets.

Companies account for tangible assets at their acquisition cost. Acquisition cost is the sum of the purchase price, shipping paid, and installation expenses if any. The acquisition cost of tangible assets is written off as *depreciation* during their usage period in the business.

Assets that do not have physical substance, such as patents, trademarks, copyrights, and goodwill, are *Intangible Assets*.

Similar to tangible assets, we account for intangible assets at their acquisition cost. *Amortization* is the method of writing off of the intangible assets' acquisition cost.

We show the depreciation and amortization as expense items in the Profit and Loss Account and reduce the assets' value to that extent in the Balance Sheet.

i) Depreciation

Assets are subject to a specific life span, called their useful life. End of the assets' useful life, the company may renovate them at an enormous cost or sell them as scrap.

Depreciation is the charge to provide for the decline in value of the tangible assets over their useful life. We write off the acquisition cost less scrap value of the tangible assets such as plant & machinery, office equipment as *depreciation*.

Methods of Depreciation

There are two methods of depreciation:

- a) Straight Line method, and
- b) Written-Down-Value method.

a) Straight Line Method

Straight Line Depreciation model		
Description		Amt USD
Asset purchase price		7,500
Shipping		200
Machine installation		150
Total cost	(i)	7,850
Useful life (years)	(ii)	5
Scrap value end of useful life	(iii)	1,800
Amount to be depreciated	iv = (I - iii)	6,050
Depreciation per year	v = (iv / iii)	1,210

We expense out an equal amount as depreciation each year under the straight-line depreciation method.

b) Written-Down Value Method

In this method, we expense out a specific percentage of the assets' written-down value every year.

Written-down value: The acquisition cost of an asset less depreciation is the asset's written-down value.

Thus, the depreciation rate applies to the written-down value each year. The depreciation charge is the highest in the first year and the lowest in the last year.

WDV depreciation method is easier to understand with a model as presented:

Written down value depreciation model	
Description	**Amt USD**
First year	
Cost	7,850
Depreciation @ 25%	(1,963)
	5,887
Second year	
Written down value	5,887
Depreciation @ 25%	(1,472)
	4,415
Third year	
Written down value	4,415
Depreciation @ 25%	(1,104)
	3,311
Fourth year	
Written down value	3,311
Depreciation @ 25%	(828)
	2,483
Fifth year	
Written down value	2,483
Depreciation @ 25%	(621)
	1,862

Choice of Depreciation Method

A question will arise in your mind—how to choose a depreciation method?

Although both methods are acceptable in Accounting, let's discuss factors that influence the choice between one depreciation method over the other.

We may distinguish assets based on their maintenance cost.

Maintenance costs of production-related assets such as plant & machinery are low when they are new. Maintenance costs increase, as they get older. For such assets, we may adopt the WDV depreciation.

Under the WDV depreciation method, the depreciation charge is higher when the assets are new during the initial years. We also know that the maintenance costs would be lower for new assets.

Thus, a higher depreciation charge during the initial years and a lower depreciation charge when the assets get older would be the better choice of a depreciation method.

Assets other than the production-related ones, such as office equipment, usually incur uniform maintenance costs during their life span. We may use the straight-line deprecation method to expense out an equal amount of depreciation every year for such assets.

Having understood the logic behind the two depreciation methods, you may choose a method depending on your business scenario. Also, choose one method for a group of assets rather than for single assets to improve simplicity in the accounting process while retaining the usability of the accounting information.

We have learned how we write off the acquisition cost of tangible assets. The next topic for our discussion is amortization.

∞

ii) Intangible Assets Amortization

Amortization is the charging-off of the acquisition cost of the intangible assets over their useful life.

Consider a company acquires a patent at a cost of twenty-five million dollars. The patent is valid for ten years. The patent value is expensed out at the rate of $2.5 million every year for ten years. Such expensing out represents the use of the patent in the business.

Goodwill

Goodwill is a special type of intangible asset. Usually, it is created in the accounting records during the business acquisition. Companies account for the excess payment as goodwill when the price paid for the business acquisition is more than the net worth. Usually, *we don't amortize goodwill.*

iii) Expenditure Amortization

In specific scenarios, expenditures incurred whose benefit accrues to the company for two or more years are carried in the Balance Sheet's assets side. We need to amortize such expenditure over the years during which the benefits accrue.

Let's learn this with an example.

Consider the dry-docking expense for ocean-going ships. Dry-docking is a major repair carried out once in five years as required by regulators.

Dry-docking repair cost once incurred, the benefit accrues for the next four years. This cost is written-off in equal installments during the four consecutive years.

Refer to the following table for an explanation of the expense amortization:

Year	Dry-docking repairs cost	Charge to expense (1/4th)
2014	300,000	75,000
2015	-	75,000
2016	-	75,000
2017	-	75,000
2018	350,000	87,500

∞

Chapter Recap

The Balance Sheet of a company provides you the following financial information:

Assets: Non-current assets and Current assets

Equity: Capital, Reserves, and Retained Earnings

Liabilities: Non-current liabilities and Current liabilities

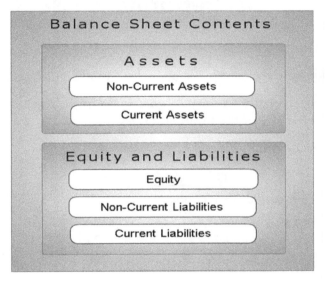

∞

In the next chapter, let's learn Profit and Loss Account, laying our foundation stronger in our pursuit of reading & interpreting the Financial Statements.

∞∞

CHAPTER 3

Profit & Loss Account —
Financial Performance Report

What is the bottom line?

You know what it means; what is the salient point?

In accounting parlance, it means 'what is the profit?' The bottom line refers to the last line of the Profit and Loss Account viz., the net Profit.

Let's understand the Profit and Loss Statement.

Chapter Contents
    1. Profit and Loss Account
    2. How to Use Profit and Loss Account

∞

1. Profit and Loss Account

Exhibit 3.1 is the model Profit and Loss Account. Exhibit 3.2 breaks down the Profit and Loss Account into its components.

Profit and Loss Account Model

Model Company			
Profit and Loss Account for the year ended 31 Dec 2014			
Description	Line no.	2014	2013
Revenue	(i)	2,163,545	2,084,534
Direct Cost			
Wages		265,482	260,945
Material cost		851,921	845,236
Other direct cost		227,838	175,638
Depreciation -machinery		77,751	71,501
Total Direct Cost	(ii)	1,422,992	1,353,320
Gross profit	iii = (i - ii)	740,553	731,214
Other Income			
Rental income	(iv)	45,000	50,000
General & Admin Expenses			
Salaries & staff cost		190,249	197,299
Office rent		47,165	40,232
Water and electricity charges		52,790	55,449
Telephone, fax & internet		28,342	22,513
Printing & stationery		18,960	17,932
Repairs & maintenance		57,983	43,984
Insurance expense		38,856	37,940
Provision for doubtful debts		5,409	6,462
Depreciation -office equipts.		2,563	2,500
Total Admin expenses	(v)	442,317	424,311
Operating Profit	vi = (iii+iv-v)	343,237	356,903
Interest on loans	(vii)	17,550	15,750
Net Profit before Taxes	viii = (vi-vii)	325,687	341,153
Taxes	(ix)	30,000	32,000
Net Profit	x = (viii-ix)	295,687	309,153
Exhibit 3.1			

Profit and Loss Account Components

Model Company

Profit and Loss Account for the year ended 31 Dec 2014

Description	Line no.	2014	2013
Revenue	(i)	2,163,545	2,084,534
Direct Cost			
Wages		265,482	260,945
Material cost		851,921	845,236
Other direct cost		227,838	175,638
Depreciation -machinery		77,751	71,501
Total Direct Cost	(ii)	1,422,992	1,353,320
Gross profit	iii = (i - ii)	**740,553**	**731,214**
Other Income			
Rental income	(iv)	45,000	50,000
General & Admin Expenses			
Salaries & staff cost		190,249	197,299
Office rent		47,165	40,232
Water and electricity charges		52,790	55,449
Telephone, fax & internet		28,342	22,513
Printing & stationery		18,960	17,932
Repairs & maintenance		57,983	43,984
Insurance expense		38,856	37,940
Provision for doubtful debts		5,409	6,462
Depreciation -office equipts.		2,563	2,500
Total Admin expenses	(v)	**442,317**	**424,311**
Net Profit before Interest and Tax (EBIT)	vi = (iii+iv-v)	**343,237**	**356,903**
Interest on loans	(vii)	17,550	15,750
Net Profit before Tax	viii = (vi-vii)	**325,687**	**341,153**
Taxes	(ix)	30,000	32,000
Net Profit	x = (viii-ix)	**295,687**	**309,153**

Exhibit 3.2

Let's discuss Profit and Loss Account by referring to the Exhibits under the topics:

- ✓ Current year values,
- ✓ Previous year values,
- ✓ Revenue,
- ✓ Direct Cost,
- ✓ Gross Profit,
- ✓ Other Income,
- ✓ General and Admin Expenses,
- ✓ Net Profit Before Interest and Tax, and
- ✓ Net Profit or Net Loss.

A. Current Year Values

We prepare the Profit and Loss Account for the 'year ended' (A). It means one year from 1 Jan 2014 to 31 Dec 2014. Thus, income and expense values for the year 2014.

Accountants refer to the year as *'Current year.'* It is the **year under financial performance review.**

B. Previous Year Values

Column (B) is income and expense values from 1 Jan 2013 to 31 Dec 2013. Column B values are for the p*revious year.*

Two-year values help us to compare the current year's performance with that of the previous year.

C. Revenue

Revenue or turnover is the income derived from selling the products or providing the services (Exhibit 3.2, C.)

Revenue is the company's gross income. *It is the top line.*

D. Direct Cost /Cost of Goods Sold

Direct Cost is the expense having direct nexus to the production activity (Exhibit 3.2, D.) We classify costs incurred in the production as direct costs. Labor costs, material costs, and production overhead are direct costs.

In a trading business, purchase costs and costs incurred in bringing the goods to the selling point, such as shipping, and insurance are direct costs.

Direct cost computed as above is the **Cost of Goods Sold (COGS).**

E. Gross Profit

The gross profit formula is:

Gross profit = Sales revenue - Direct Cost

Refer to (E) for the gross profit in the model Profit and Loss Account Exhibit 3.2.

GP Ratio

The gross profit ratio is the percentage of gross profit to sales revenue. This measure is crucial as it relates to the *business model.*

The company's business plan should specify the GP Ratio range as a benchmark. Comparative analysis of the actual GP Ratio with that of the company's business plan provides a good performance measure.

Please refer to the Chapter 7 Ratio Analysis for further discussion on GP Ratio (page no. 63.)

F. Other Income

Most companies have peripheral activities. Whereas we treat sales income from core business function as revenue, income from peripheral or non-core business activities is its 'other income' (Exhibit 3.2, F.)

Example: Income from renting out a portion of an office building owned by the company is its 'other income.'

G. General and Admin Expenses

General and Admin Expenses are *expenses incurred to run* the company (G.) We also call these expenses as 'general and admin overhead.'

For a narrow range of activity levels (page 5), general and admin overhead do not change. General and admin overhead include salaries and staff-related costs, rent for office, printing and stationery, telephone and the internet, audit, and office maintenance cost.

H. Net Profit before Interest and Tax

EBIT (marked 'H') reveals Profit from the business. For the EBIT computation, we exclude the financing cost and income tax.

Monitoring actual EBIT with the budgeted EBIT is the responsibility of the Operations Manager or the General Manager.

I. Net Profit or Loss

Net profit (Exhibit 3.2, I) is the final amount left of the revenue after meeting all expenses and tax on income. It is the last line in the Profit and Loss account. *It is the bottom-line.*

You can improve the bottom line with sound short-term operational and long-term investment decisions—the topics that we will learn later in this book.

The percentage of *net profit to revenue* is the second important measure of profitability after GP Ratio. Depending on the industry, these ratios differ.

We'll discuss NP Ratios (page no. 66) under Chapter 7 Ratio Analysis.

∞

2. How to Use Profit and Loss Account

Companies prepare *year-end* Profit and Loss Account for the internal management and the external stakeholders such as banks, financial institutions, and owners.

The Profit and Loss Account covered so far *in this chapter* is the year-end model. Companies also prepare the Profit and Loss Accounts monthly. Managers monitor their company's financial performance with the monthly Profit and Loss Account.

The monthly Profit and Loss Account formats are flexible. We'll discuss them under Chapter 6, Monitoring Financial Performance (page no. 53.)

∞

Chapter Recap

Profit and Loss Account reveals the financial performance of a company. Profit and Loss A/c comprise:

- ✓ Revenue,
- ✓ Direct Cost,
- ✓ Other Income,
- ✓ General & Admin Overhead cost, and
- ✓ Net Profit or Loss.

∞

In the last two chapters, we learned Balance Sheet and Profit and Loss Account. Let's learn **Cash Flow Statement** in the next chapter.

∞∞∞

CHAPTER 4

Cash Flow Statement —

Where Is The Cash?

The Cash Flow Statement shows where we made money and where we spent between two dates.

So, what is the importance of the Cash Flow Statement?

Cash is King is by no means an understatement. The success or failure of a business depends significantly on how the company optimally deploys its cash resources.

Concisely, the Cash Flow Statement enables managers to fine-tune the company's funding strategies.

Chapter Contents

1. Cash Flow Statement
2. Cash from Operations
3. Cash Flows from Investment Activities
4. Cash Flows from Financing Activities
5. Reconciliation

∞

1. Cash Flow Statement

We prepare a Cash Flow Statement for one year.

We have Exhibit 4.1 to explain the Cash Flow Statement with current year values from 1 Jan 2014 to 31 Dec 2014 and the corresponding previous year values.

The Cash Flow Statement shows:

> i) Cash from operations,
>
> ii) Cash flows from investing activities, and
>
> iii) Cash flows from financing activities.

Managers gain better insight by classifying the cash movements under the above business activities.

Model Company
Cash flow statement for the year ended 31 Dec 2014

Description	Line no.	2014	2013
A. CASH FROM OPERATIONS			
Net profit as per Profit & Loss a/c		295,687	309,153
Add back			
Depreciation in Admin & General cost		2,563	2,500
Depreciation in Direct Cost		77,751	71,501
Interest on loans		17,550	15,750
Taxes		30,000	32,000
A.1 Cash profit		*423,550*	*430,904*
Adjustments for Working Capital			
Changes in inventories		(25,577)	(39,615)
Changes in trade and other receivables		(92,325)	(10,574)
Changes in trade and other payables		(1,617)	20,768
A.2 Cash from operations		*304,031*	*401,483*
Less: Interest on loans		(17,550)	(15,750)
Less: Taxes		(30,000)	(32,000)
A.3 Net cash from operations	(i)	*256,481*	*353,733*
B. CASH FLOWS FROM INVESTING ACTIVITIES			
Land addition		-	(75,000)
Furniture additions		(2,500)	-
Plant & Machinery additions		(100,000)	-
Net cash (used in) investing activities	(ii)	*(102,500)*	*(75,000)*
C. CASH FLOWS FROM FINANCING ACTIVITIES			
Borrowing		300,000	
Repayment of loan		(195,000)	(150,000)
Dividend / profit payout		(250,000)	(100,000)
Sub total	(iii)	*(145,000)*	*(250,000)*
RECONCILIATION			
Net changes in cash (iv = i+ii+iii)		8,981	28,733
Cash -Beginning balance		96,679	67,946
Cash -Ending balance		105,660	96,679

Exhibit 4.1

∞

2. Cash from Operations

Model Company
Cash flow statement for the year ended 31 Dec 2014

Description	Line no.	2014	2013
A. CASH FROM OPERATIONS			
Net profit as per Profit & Loss a/c ①		295,687	309,153
Add back *From Profit and Loss Account*			
Depreciation in Admin & General cost		2,003	2,500
Depreciation in Direct Cost		77,751	71,501
Interest on loans ② Added now		17,550	15,750
Taxes		30,000	32,000
③ *A.1 Cash profit*		423,550	430,904
Adjustments for Working Capital			
Changes in inventories		(25,577)	(39,615)
Changes in trade and other receivables		(92,325)	(10,574)
Changes in trade and other payables		(1,617)	20,768
④ *A.2 Cash from operations*		304,031	401,483
Less: Interest on loans ⑤ Deducted now		(17,550)	(15,750)
Less: Taxes		(30,000)	(32,000)
A.3 Net cash from operations (i) ⑥		256,481	353,733
B. CASH FLOWS FROM INVESTING ACTIVITIES			
Land addition		-	(75,000)
Furniture additions		(2,500)	-
Plant & Machinery additions		(100,000)	-
Net cash (used in) investing activities (ii)		(102,500)	(75,000)
C. CASH FLOWS FROM FINANCING ACTIVITIES			
Borrowing		300,000	
Repayment of loan		(195,000)	(150,000)
Dividend / profit payout		(250,000)	(100,000)
Sub total (iii)		(145,000)	(250,000)
RECONCILIATION			
Net changes in cash (iv = i+ii+iii)		8,981	28,733
Cash -Beginning balance		96,679	67,946
Cash -Ending balance		105,660	96,679

Exhibit 4.2

Cash from operations shows the cash movements arising from purchases, production, sales, and related expenses.

Beginning with 'Net Profit as per Profit and Loss a/c,' we present 'Cash from Operations' in three stages:

> A.1 Cash Profit,
> A.2 Cash from Operations, and
> A.3 Net Cash from Operations.

A.1 Cash Profit

We compute Cash Profit (marked 3) from Net Profit by adding back:

> Depreciation and amortization being non-cash expenses,
> Interest paid on loans (marked 2), and
> Income tax (marked 2).

When the Profit and Loss Account shows a net loss, the next vital measure to watch is cash profit.

Please be reminded that 'Cash is King.'

Negative cash profit (cash loss) reveals a critical financial situation—the Company cannot meet its running costs from its internal cash generation.

The Company is losing money in the short term. It requires external funding either as borrowings or as loans from the owners to continue the business activities.

The company needs operational and strategic corrective measures to stop incurring further cash losses and turnaround.

The turnaround measures can be:

- ✓ Improved working capital management (attention required: inventory may build up beyond what is needed, customers are not paying up in time);
- ✓ Re-visit fixed cost commitments such as rent, salaries; and
- ✓ Re-visit business model/ strategy for the product costing and their pricing.

A.2 Cash from Operations

Cash from operations (refer to 4) is the cash profit adjusted for *cash effects of changes in working capital.*

Changes in Working Capital

Net of current assets and current liabilities is the working capital. Current assets include inventories and customers' balances; current liabilities include vendors' balances.

This part of the Cash Flow statement reveals an increase or decrease in cash because of the changes in working capital.

Please refer to Chapter 8, Working Capital Management (page no. 80), for further discussion.

A.3 Net Cash from Operations

We deduct interest paid on loans and income tax (refer to 5) from cash from operations to get the net cash from operations.

Net cash from operations (6) is the *amount available for investments such as replacing worn-out plant and machinery, buying new machinery.*

∞

3. Cash Flows from Investment Activities

Model Company
Cash flow statement for the year ended 31 Dec 2014

Description	Line no.	2014	2013
A. CASH FROM OPERATIONS			
Net profit as per Profit & Loss a/c		295,687	309,153
Add back			
Depreciation in Admin & General cost		2,563	2,500
Depreciation in Direct Cost		77,751	71,501
Interest on loans		17,550	15,750
Taxes		30,000	32,000
A.1 Cash profit		*423,550*	*430,904*
Adjustments for Working Capital			
Changes in inventories		(25,577)	(39,615)
Changes in trade and other receivables		(92,325)	(10,574)
Changes in trade and other payables		(1,617)	20,768
A.2 Cash from operations		*304,031*	*401,483*
Less: Interest on loans		(17,550)	(15,750)
Less: Taxes		(30,000)	(32,000)
A.3 Net cash from operations	(i)	256,481	353,733
B. CASH FLOWS FROM INVESTING ACTIVITIES			
Land addition		-	(75,000)
Furniture additions		(2,500)	-
Plant & Machinery additions		(100,000)	-
Net cash (used in) investing activities	(ii)	(102,500)	(75,000)
C. CASH FLOWS FROM FINANCING ACTIVITIES			
Borrowing		300,000	
Repayment of loan		(195,000)	(150,000)
Dividend / profit payout		(250,000)	(100,000)
Sub total	(iii)	(145,000)	(250,000)
RECONCILIATION			
Net changes in cash (iv = i+ii+iii)		8,981	28,733
Cash -Beginning balance		96,679	67,946
Cash -Ending balance		105,660	96,679

Exhibit 4.3

Investment activities mean purchases and sales of non-current assets. Thus, cash movements for the purchases of new assets and sales of worn-out, unused, or outdated assets (marked 7) are summarized under this heading.

Negative values in the model indicate cash payments for assets purchase.

∞

4. Cash Flows from Financing Activities

Business needs funding to carry on its activities. Companies secure funds through owners' contributions and borrowings.

This part of the Cash Flow Statement shows cash movements from the funding activities (marked 8.) Funding activities are new shares issued, dividend paid, loan raised, and repayment of loans.

5. Reconciliation

You may skip this topic.

The information presented under reconciliation does not influence managers' decision-making.

But if you are curious to know how the cash movements are reconciled with the Cash and Bank Balances in the Balance Sheet, continue reading.

Reconciliation ensures arithmetical accuracy of the Financial Statements.

Now, refer to Exhibit 4.4 for a visual presentation of the reconciliation.

Reconciliation — a visual presentation

Model Company Cash flow statement for the year ended 31 Dec 2014			
Description	Line no.	2014	2013
A. CASH FROM OPERATIONS			
Net profit as per Profit & Loss a/c		295,687	309,153
Add back			
Depreciation in Admin & General cost		2,563	2,500
Depreciation in Direct Cost		77,751	71,501
Interest on loans		17,550	15,750
Taxes		30,000	32,000
A.1 Cash profit		*423,550*	*430,904*
Adjustments for Working Capital			
Changes in inventories		(25,577)	(39,615)
Changes in trade and other receivables		(92,325)	(10,574)
Changes in trade and other payables		(1,617)	20,768
A.2 Cash from operations		*304,031*	*401,483*
Less: Interest on loans		(17,550)	(15,750)
Less: Taxes		(30,000)	(32,000)
A.3 Net cash from operations	(i)	256,481	353,733
B. CASH FLOWS FROM INVESTING ACTIVITIES			
Land addition		-	(75,000)
Furniture additions		(2,500)	-
Plant & Machinery additions		(100,000)	-
Net cash (used in) investing activities	(ii)	(102,500)	(75,000)
C. CASH FLOWS FROM FINANCING ACTIVITIES			
Borrowing		300,000	
Repayment of loan	Cash & Bank balance from Balance Sheet	(195,000)	(150,000)
Dividend / profit payout		(250,000)	(100,000)
Sub total	(iii)	(145,000)	(250,000)
RECONCILIATION			
9 *Net changes in cash* (iv = i+ii+iii)		8,981	28,733
Cash -Beginning balance	**10**	96,679	67,946
Cash -Ending balance	**11**	105,660	96,679
Exhibit 4.4			

We have seen cash movements during the year and corresponding previous year, classified and listed in the cash flow statement.

The net amount of cash from operating, investing, and financing activities is the 'Net changes in cash' (9.)

Amount marked (10) is the cash and bank balance at the year beginning as below:

> USD 67,946 is as of 1 Jan 2013, and
>
> USD 96,679 is the balance as of 1 Jan 2014.

Amount marked (11) is the cash and bank balance at the year-end:

> USD 96,679 is the balance as of 31 Dec 2013, and
>
> USD 105,660 is as of 31 Dec 2014.

Please revisit Exhibit 2.1—model Balance Sheet to see these values listed against *Cash and Bank*.

Thus, we matched the sum of cash movements in the Cash Flow Statement with the Balance Sheet Cash & Bank values.

∞

Chapter Recap

A company has to deploy its cash resources optimally. The Cash Flow Statement presents vital cash movement information to help managers fine-tune the *company's financing strategies.*

Cash Flow Statement highlights cash movements from

i) Cash from operations,

ii) Cash flows from investing activities, and

iii) Cash flows from financing activities.

∞

In the last three chapters, we have learned how a company's financial information is presented in the Balance Sheet, the Profit and Loss Account, and the Cash Flow Statement.

We will learn how to read and interpret financial statements in the next three chapters.

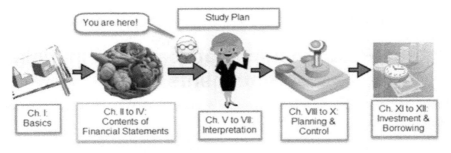

∞∞

CHAPTER 5

Demystify Financial Statements

Reading and interpreting financial statements may sound complicated, but a systematic approach would make it easier.

As a first step to understanding the financial statements and using them for decision-making, we'll learn *how to read them* in this chapter.

Chapter Contents

1. The Relationships between the Financial Statements
2. Understand how each line item relates to other items within the financial statements
3. The Business Perspective

1. The Relationships between the Financial Statements

Financial statements relate to each other, and you should *read them together* to form an opinion on them.

Let's learn the relationships under the following topics:

i) Cash Flow Statement and Profit and Loss Account,

ii) Cash Flow Statement and Balance Sheet, and

iii) Balance Sheet and Profit and Loss Account.

i) Cash Flow Statement & Profit and Loss Account

Let's now grasp how the values of these two financial statements relate to each other. Please refer to Exhibit 5.1 Profit and Loss Account and Exhibit 5.2 Cash Flow Statement.

A portion of the statements is hidden for presentation purposes, but this won't affect our study now.

Model Company

Profit and Loss Account for the year ended 31st Dec 2014

Description	Line no.	2014	2013
Revenue	(i)	2,163,545	2,084,534
Direct Cost			
Wages		265,482	260,945
Material cost		851,921	845,236
Other direct cost		227,838	175,638
Depreciation -machinery		77,751	71,501
Total Direct Cost	(ii)	1,422,992	1,353,320
Repairs & maintenance		57,983	43,984
Insurance expense		38,856	37,940
Provision for doubtful debts		5,409	6,462
Depreciation -office equipts.		2,563	2,500
Total Admin expenses	(v)	442,317	424,311
Operating Profit	(iii+iv-v)	343,237	356,903
Interest on loans	(vii)	17,550	15,750
Net Pr	viii = (vi-vii)	325,687	341,153
Taxes		30,000	32,000
Net Profit	x = (viii-ix)	295,687	309,153

Non-cash expense added to Net profit ②

Non-cash expense added to Net profit ②

Interest & Taxes added to get 'Cash Profit' ③

Cash Flow Statement begins with Net profit for the year ①

Exhibit 5.1

Model Company
Cash flow statement for the year ended 31st Dec 2014

Description	Line no.	2014	2013
A. CASH FROM OPERATIONS			
Net profit as per Profit & Loss a/c	①	295,687	309,153
Add back			
Depreciation in Admin & General cost	②	2,563	2,500
Depreciation in Direct Cost		77,751	71,501
Interest on loans		17,550	15,750
Taxes	③	30,000	32,000
A.1 Cash profit		423,550	430,904
Adjustments for Working Capital			
Changes in inventories		(25,577)	(39,615)
Changes in trade and other receivables		(92,325)	(10,574)
Changes in trade and other payables		(1,617)	20,768
A.2 Cash from operations		304,031	401,483
Less: Interest on loans	④	(17,550)	(15,750)
Less: Taxes		(30,000)	(32,000)
A.3 Net cash from operations	(i)	256,481	353,733
B. CASH FLOWS FROM INVESTING			
Cash -Beginning balance		96,679	67,946
Cash -Ending balance		105,660	96,679

Exhibit 5.2

a) Net Profit from Profit and Loss Account

Profit and Loss Account shows the net results: net profit or a net loss. The Cash Flow Statement *begins with the P & L A/c net profit or net loss* value (marked 1 in both the Exhibits.)

We know the P & L A/c is drawn based on the accrual accounting (page no. 3) principle. We begin with the accrual accounting-based net profit or loss and make changes in the Cash Flow Statement to nullify those accrual adjustments. We reverse the accrual concept adjustments to study the cash movements.

b) Depreciation from Profit and Loss Account

We know depreciation is an expense but not a cash payment. Therefore, we add back the Profit and Loss Account depreciation expense in the Cash Flow Statement to compute the cash flows resulting from business operations (marked 2.)

c) Interest and Income Tax

Interest and income tax in the Profit and Loss Account are cash expenses (marked 3.) However, they are not expenses for running the business operations. So, we add them back to get the *Cash Profit*.

Later, we deduct both items from cash profit to derive *Net Cash from Operations*.

Please refer to our discussions on Cash Profit, Cash from Operations, and Net Cash from Operations topics under 'Cash from Operations' (page no. 38) under Chapter 4, Cash Flow Statement.

∞

ii) Cash Flow Statement and Balance Sheet

Let's learn how the Balance Sheet values relate to the Cash Flow Statement values.

We are going to dissect the Cash Flow Statement components to understand the relationships.

Exhibit 5.3 depicts the extract of the Cash Flow Statement and Exhibit 5.4 that of Balance Sheet highlighting the relationships between the two financial statements visually.

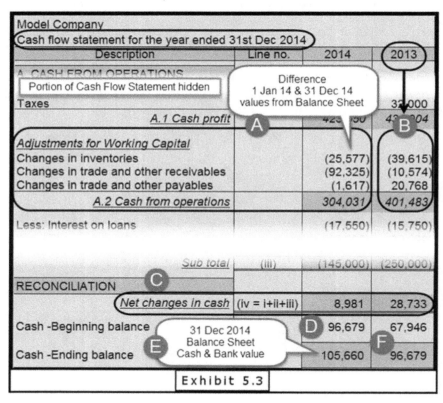

Exhibit 5.3

Model Company			
Balance Sheet as at 31st Dec 2014			
Description	Line no.	2014 (Current year)	2013 (Previous year)
Current assets			
Inventory G		350,988	325,411
Trade and other receivables		401,855	310,879
Other current assets		12,819	11,470
Cash & bank		105,660	96,679
Total current assets	(ii)	871,322	744,439
Total assets	iii = (i+ii)	1,542,515	1,393,445
EQUITY & LIABILITIES			
Equity			
Total equity & liabilities	vii = (iv+v+vi)	1,542,515	1,393,445
	Exhibit 5.4		

Ending Cash balance in Cash Flow Statement (E)

Ending Cash balance (F)

i) Adjustments for Working Capital (A)

Current Assets & Current Liabilities in the Balance Sheets make up a company's working capital (page no. 80.) We present cash movements resulting from changes in individual components of current assets (*excluding cash & bank*) and current liabilities under 'Adjustments for Working Capital' (Exhibit 5.3, A & Exhibit 5.4, G.)

Example: Adjustment for changes in inventory values:

$ 325,411 as on 31 Dec 2013 & $ 350,988 as on 31 Dec 2014

Thus, inventory values increase by $ 25,577.

The increase in inventory happens through cash payment. Thus the cash outflow is shown as the negative value -$25,577 in the cash flow statement. Negative value refers to cash payment.

ii) Cash Flows from Investing Activities (B)

Investment activities in the context of the Cash Flow Statement refer to buying and selling non-current assets (page no. 13) such as land, building, plant & machinery.

Thus, we present cash movements arising from non-current assets in the Balance Sheet under *Cash Flows from Investing Activities* in the Cash Flow Statement.

iii) Cash Flows from Financing Activities (C)

A company finances its business operations with owners' equity and borrowed funds (non-current liabilities.) We summarize cash receipts and cash payments of 'equity and non-current liabilities' under the heading *Cash Flows from Financing Activities*.

The mathematics behind this computation is straightforward. We calculate the difference between equity and non-current liabilities components of the two dates—1 Jan 2014 and 31 Dec 2014 and present the same in the Cash Flow Statement.

iv) Reconciliation

Beginning cash balance (on 1 Jan 2014—marked D) and ending cash balance (on 31 Dec 2014—labeled E) are from *Cash & Bank* in the Balance Sheet (H.) The difference between the beginning and ending balances is equal to Net Changes in Cash Balance.

Thus, we match the Cash Flow Statement values with that of Balance Sheet cash and bank values.

∞

iii) Balance Sheet and Profit and Loss Account

Profit and Loss Account—Net Profit is the amount left after all expenses are charged against revenue. Net Profit belongs to the owners of the company. Thus, net profit, after dividend distribution, is added to Retained Earnings Account at the year-end. Retained Earnings are part of Equity in the Balance Sheet: net profit increases and net loss decrease owners' equity.

∞

2. How Each Value Relates to Other Values

Any of the Balance Sheet items by themselves provide limited information. Consider the 'inventory' value.

Is the company's inventory too high?

You can answer this question by relating the inventory value to the **cost of goods sold**.

Let us understand the relationship between inventory and the cost of goods sold.

The purpose of the inventory is to feed the sales line. Thus, it has a relationship to sales. We know sales have two components: cost and profit margin. However, the profit margin component in sales has no relationship to the inventory value. Hence, we ignore the profit margin in sales and consider only the cost component, viz., cost of goods sold, for the study of inventory value.

The inventory turnover ratio explains the above relationship.

Ratios explain the relationship between related items of financial statements. We will discuss the relationships under Chapter 7 Ratio Analysis (page no. 62.)

∞

3. The Business Perspective

The business perspective is the high-level overview of the business model, strategy, market dynamics, industry knowledge, and the general economic outlook.

In the backdrop of business perspective, ratio analysis provides valuable insight—if the values under review are at their optimum levels.

Example: Inventory, Sales, and Customer Satisfaction

The company keeps inventory to fulfill customer orders. Thus, the company determines the inventory size that maximizes customer satisfaction by timely delivery and minimizes loss because of overstocking.

Also, the required inventory is based on the projected sales and the time for raw materials to finished goods conversion.

The above factors are industry-specific. For example, in textile showrooms—customer satisfaction is maximized with enough trending merchandise in the stores.

Chapter Recap

The three financial statements are interrelated.

Understanding the relationship between the Balance Sheet, Profit, and Loss Account and the Cash Flow Statement and the relationship between items in those statements helps us interpret the financial information.

We use the mathematical ratios at the backdrop of business perspective for this purpose.

The next two chapters, Chapter 6 Monitoring Financial Performance and Chapter 7 Ratio Analysis, are only extensions of the current chapter, 'Demystify Financial Statements.' However, I kept them as separate chapters because of their relative importance.

Continue reading.

∞∞

CHAPTER 6

Monitoring Financial Performance

You are part of the management responsible for the financial performance of your company! You don't want surprises when you read the year-end Profit and Loss Account. You want to monitor the financial performance.

You monitor financial performance with Management Information System Reports.

MIS reports are the reports with financial and non-financial information, prepared and presented periodically by the finance and operations team for the benefit of the management in its pursuit to direct & lead the business.

MIS reports include detailed quantity reports, costing reports, and financial information with graphical presentations depending on the industry, the business model, and the unique requirements.

The MIS reports for finance have the basic format of Profit and Loss Account.

MIS reports are prepared month on month, internal, redesigned as often as required, and are available in multiple presentation formats to serve the individual company's business environment. It is a flexible reporting format to **help the managers** in their decision-making roles.

As we understand now, MIS reports include a wide variety of reports. We will cover the Profit and Loss Account format in this chapter.

Profit and Loss Account in an MIS Report helps the management identify and focus on deviations from the planned performance.

There are several methods of presentation of financial information in an MIS report. As the purpose of this report is to identify deviations and show abnormal behaviors of any group of expense or income accounts, all the methods compare the current month (latest month) data with the rest of the financial data already available such as historical performance and budget.

Chapter Contents

1. Comparison with Budget
2. Comparison with Previous Months
3. Common Size Statement
4. Comparison with Previous Year Values
5. Comparison with Averages
6. Choosing Between Different Methods

∞

1. Comparison with Budget

In this format, budget values act as the benchmark.

Managers investigate abnormal deviations of actual from the budgeted values. This exercise provides the managers a sound basis for taking corrective actions where necessary.

Exhibit 6.1 shows a model MIS report with budget and variance columns.

Model Company
Profit and Loss Account for the year ended 31 Dec 2014

| Description | 2014 | | Variance | | Favorable/ |
	Actual	Budget	Amount	Percentage	Unfavorable
Revenue	2,163,545	2,100,000	63,545	3.0%	Favorable
Direct Cost					
Wages	265,482	260,000	-5,482	-2.1%	Unfavorable
Material cost	851,921	800,000	-51,921	-6.5%	Unfavorable
Other direct cost	227,838	230,000	2,162	0.9%	Favorable
Depreciation	77,751	77,750	-1	0.0%	
Total Direct Cost	**1,422,992**	**1,367,750**	**-55,242**	**-4.0%**	Unfavorable
Gross profit	**740,553**	**732,250**	**8,303**	**1.1%**	Favorable
Other Income					
Rental income	45,000	45,000	0	0.0%	
General & Admin Expenses					
Salaries & staff cost	190,249	190,000	-249	-0.1%	
Office rent	47,165	47,000	-165	-0.4%	
Water and electricity charges	52,790	54,000	1,210	2.2%	Favorable
Telephone, fax & internet	28,342	28,000	-342	-1.2%	
Printing & stationery	18,960	17,500	-1,460	-8.3%	Unfavorable
Repairs & maintenance	57,983	50,000	-7,983	-16.0%	Unfavorable
Insurance expense	38,856	38,900	44	0.1%	
Provision for doubtful debts	5,409	2,500	-2,909	-116.4%	Unfavorable
Depreciation	2,563	2,600	38	1.4%	
Total Admin expenses	**442,317**	**430,500**	**-11,817**	**-2.7%**	Unfavorable
Operating Profit	**343,237**	**346,750**	**-3,514**	**-1.0%**	Unfavorable
Interest on loans	17,550	17,500	50	0.3%	
Net Profit before Taxes	**325,687**	**329,250**	**-3,564**	**-1.1%**	Unfavorable
Taxes	30,000	30,000	0	0.0%	
Net Profit	295,687	299,250	-3,564	-1.2%	Unfavorable
	Exhibit 6.1				

Variance is the difference between actual and budget values. As formulae:

$$\text{Income Variance} = \text{Actual} - \text{Budget}$$

$$\text{Expense Variance} = \text{Budget} - \text{Actual}$$

Actual and budget values are presented with both variances in amount and variance as a percentage.

Abnormal Deviations

Revenue is higher by three percent. However, increased material costs of 6.5% offset the revenue increase, resulting in only a 1.1% increase in the Gross Profit.

In the General and Admin Expenses, Repairs and Maintenance and Provision for Doubtful Debts have unfavorable variances, resulting in reduced net Profit.

The report enables the management to investigate the increase in material costs, repair costs, and doubtful debts and take corrective actions.

∞

2. Comparison with Previous Months

Let us consider the Profit and Loss Account for three months—January, February, and March 2014 shown in Exhibit 6.2. We study the March 2014 values with the two previous months' values, viz. January & February 2014.

Model Company			
Profit and Loss account for the quarter ending 31st Mar 2014			
Description	31-Jan-14	28-Feb-14	31-Mar-14
Revenue	185,295	182,295	183,295
Direct Cost			
Wages	22,123	22,023	22,523
Material cost	72,993	70,993	76,200
Other direct cost	19,126	19,200	18,586
Depreciation	6,479	6,479	6,479
Total Direct Cost	**120,721**	**118,695**	**123,788**
Gross profit	**64,574**	**63,600**	**59,507**
Other Income			
Rent income	3,750	3,750	3,750
General & Admin Expenses			
Salaries & staff cost	16,054	15,854	15,954
Office rent	3,930	3,930	3,930
Water and electricity charges	4,422	4,390	4,450
Telephone, fax & internet	2,400	2,520	2,395
Printing & stationery	1,400	1,700	1,550
Repairs & maintenance	5,122	5,300	8,500
Insurance expense	3,238	3,238	3,238
Provision for doubtful debts	450	450	450
Depreciation	213	213	213
Total Admin expenses	**37,229**	**37,595**	**40,680**
Operating Profit	**31,095**	**29,755**	**22,577**
Interest on loans	1,462	1,462	1,462
Net Profit before Taxes	**29,633**	**28,293**	**21,115**
Taxes	2,500	2,500	2,500
Net Profit	**27,133**	**25,793**	**18,615**
	Exhibit 6.2		

Higher material cost

Higher repairs cost

From a comparison, we observe a hike in material costs under direct costs and an increase in repairs and maintenance expenses under admin overhead, as highlighted.

Thus, comparing current month values with previous year values enables the managers to go beyond the numbers and determine the reasons behind this adverse change affecting gross profit and net profit.

Let's study the same values under the common-size statement model in the next subtopic.

∞

3. Common-Size Statement

In this model, we present Profit and Loss Account values as percentages against revenue. Refer to the Common-Size Statement for the same Profit and Loss account in Exhibit 6.3.

Model Company			
Profit and Loss account, common size statement			
Description	Jan-14	Feb-14	Mar-14
Revenue	100.00%	100.00%	100.00%
Direct Cost		Higher material cost in %	
Wages	11.94%	12.08%	12.29%
Material cost	39.39%	38.94%	41.57%
Other direct cost	10.32%	10.53%	10.14%
Depreciation	3.50%	3.55%	3.53%
Total Direct Cost	65.15%	65.11%	67.53%
Gross profit	34.85%	34.89%	32.47%
Other Income			
Rent income	2.02%	2.06%	2.05%
General & Admin Expenses		Higher repairs cost in %	
Salaries & staff cost	8.66%	8.70%	8.70%
Office rent	2.12%	2.16%	2.14%
Water and electricity charges	2.39%	2.41%	2.43%
Telephone, fax & internet	1.30%	1.38%	1.31%
Printing & stationery	0.76%	0.93%	0.85%
Repairs & maintenance	2.76%	2.91%	4.64%
Insurance expense	1.75%	1.78%	1.77%
Provision for doubtful debts	0.24%	0.25%	0.25%
Depreciation	0.11%	0.12%	0.12%
Total Admin expenses	20.09%	20.62%	22.19%
Operating Profit	16.78%	16.32%	12.32%
Interest on loans	0.79%	0.80%	0.80%
Net Profit before Taxes	15.99%	15.52%	11.52%
Taxes	1.35%	1.37%	1.36%
Net Profit	14.64%	14.15%	10.16%
	Exhibit 6.3		

From the example given above, we see net profit is showing a significant drop for the month under study, Mar 2014. Further analysis reveals an increase in the materials and repairs cost.

We can investigate further to find out the reasons for the cost increase and take suitable remedial measures.

∞

4. Comparison with Previous Year Values

This method presents a comparison of Profit and Loss account values with that of the previous year's same period values. For example, we compare Jan 2014 values with Jan 2013 values.

5. Comparison with Averages

Consider the Profit and Loss account for Jun 2014. It is the 6th-month statement (the year begins 1 Jan 2014). We present Jun 2014 values alongside averages of six months, Jan 2014 to Jun 2014.

If your business is free from seasonal fluctuations, then averages provide an excellent comparison to highlight the deviations and enable you to judge the trend.

∞

6. Choosing Between Different Methods

Suppose your company has an established budget exercise. In that case, comparing income and expense values of the period under review with the corresponding budget values provides a sound basis for further investigation and suitable corrective actions.

If you don't have the budget values, you can use the current values vs. the same period of last year's values comparison method.

∞

Chapter Recap

MIS Profit and Loss Account reports are prepared for the benefit of the company's managers. The MIS report formats vary between companies depending on the type of industry and the availability of past Profit and Loss Account information and budget values.

MIS reports compare the current performance with budget or previous period values to highlight the **exceptions and abnormal deviations.** The formats include:

- ✓ Comparison with the annual budget,
- ✓ Comparison with previous months, and
- ✓ Common-size statement.

You choose the format that best serves the purpose on hand — monitoring financial performance.

∞

In the next chapter, we will see how financial ratios help you further in interpreting Financial Statements.

∞∞∞

CHAPTER 7

Ratio Analysis —

Finding the Root Cause

I can't change the direction of the wind, but I can adjust my sails always to reach my destination -Jimmy Dean

Gaining insight is not accidental but happens by intelligent action.

∞

We analyze the related values in the Balance Sheet and Profit and Loss account using mathematical ratios in our pursuit to read and interpret financial statements.

A ratio is a mathematical relationship between the two related values. Ratios calculated for associated data items provide significantly helpful information. Ratio analysis is the commonly used tool for drawing insight into financial information.

An example will make this clear. The net profit ratio reveals the profit margin for every dollar of sales value.

Ratio analysis is the tool available for the management to evaluate financial performance. Ratio analysis helps a company inculcate financial discipline into its culture.

Financial ratios provide valuable information, help you ask further questions, draw conclusions, and help make financially prudent decisions. Ratios empower you to go beyond the symptoms and find out the root cause for the symptoms.

Chapter Contents

∞

1. Profitability Ratios

You can measure profitability with

    i) Gross Profit Ratio,

    ii) Net Profit Ratio, and

    iii) Asset Turnover Ratio.

i) Gross Profit Ratio

GP Ratio is the first measure of profitability for a company.

Gross Profit (page no.30) is the amount remaining after deducting the direct costs from revenue.

GP Ratio defines the relationship between gross profit and revenue. Refer to Exhibit 7.1 for the GP ratio formula.

Ratio / Year		2014	2013	Formula
Gross Profit Ratio		34%	35%	= (Gross profit / Revenue) x 100
Where				
Gross Profit	=	740,553	731,214	Values from
Revenue	=	2,163,545	2,084,534	'Model Profit & Loss a/c' (Chapter III)
			Exhibit 7.1	

Exhibit 7.2 (marked A) explains the Profit and Loss Account values to help you grasp the idea behind the GP ratio and NP ratio formulae.

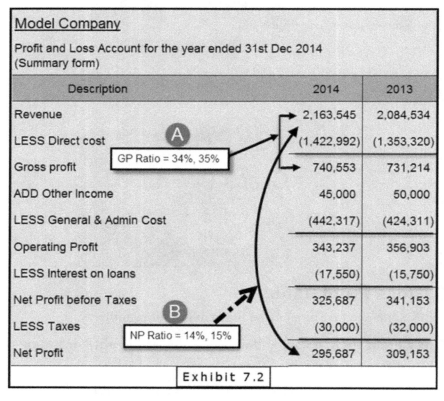

Model Company

Profit and Loss Account for the year ended 31st Dec 2014
(Summary form)

Description	2014	2013
Revenue	2,163,545	2,084,534
LESS Direct cost	(1,422,992)	(1,353,320)
Gross profit	740,553	731,214
ADD Other Income	45,000	50,000
LESS General & Admin Cost	(442,317)	(424,311)
Operating Profit	343,237	356,903
LESS Interest on loans	(17,550)	(15,750)
Net Profit before Taxes	325,687	341,153
LESS Taxes	(30,000)	(32,000)
Net Profit	295,687	309,153

GP Ratio = 34%, 35%

NP Ratio = 14%, 15%

Exhibit 7.2

GP Ratio of thirty-four percent means that the company makes thirty-four cents gross profit after meeting sixty-six cents direct cost for every dollar of revenue.

We can compute GP Ratio for a small business, or division of a large company, or a corporate entity—having multiple productions and selling activities.

Comparison of the GP Ratio with that of the competitor provides valuable information about the company's competitiveness.

GP Ratio is highly industry sensitive. We know the direct costs incurred to earn rental income in a real estate business are significantly low compared to that of the manufacturing and selling business model. Therefore, we compare GP ratios of two divisions or companies only when they operate in the same industry.

How revenue relates to gross profit?

The gross profit increases at a higher rate when there is an increase in revenue. This is because of the cost behavior, some costs are fixed, and some are variable.

Variable and Fixed Costs

Most of the direct costs increase with an increase in production. Raw material costs, direct labor costs, and electricity for running the machinery are examples that increase with an increase in production volume. These costs are *variable direct costs*.

However, not every direct cost changes with a change in production. For example, depreciation on production assets, though direct cost, remains unchanged irrespective of changes in production level. We refer to such expenses as *fixed direct costs*.

Thus, both variable and fixed costs make up the total direct costs.

Therefore, gross profit increases significantly for a slight increase in revenue and vice versa—depending on the proportion of the fixed costs to the total costs.

Illustration:

Revenue	$10,000
Fixed direct costs	$4,000
Variable direct costs	$3,000
Gross profit	$3,000

Now, consider 5% increase in revenue.

Revenue	$10,500 (5% increase)
Fixed direct costs	$4,000
Variable direct costs	$3,150 (5% increase)
Gross profit	3,350 (11.7% increase)

Thus, for a 5% increase in sales, there is an 11.7% increase in gross profit. This is because of the fixed direct cost component in the total direct costs.

ii) Net Profit Ratio

NP Ratio or the net margin is the ratio between net profit and revenue. Please refer to Exhibit 7.3 & 'B' in Exhibit 7.2.

Ratio / Year		2014	2013	Formula
Net Profit Ratio		14%	15%	= (Net profit / Revenue) x 100
Where				
Net Profit	=	295,687	309,153	Values from
Revenue	=	2,163,545	2,084,534	'Model Profit & Loss a/c' (Chapter III)
			Exhibit 7.3	

General and Admin Expenses (page no.31) are deducted from gross profit to compute the net Profit.

NP Ratio of fourteen percent shows that the company is making fourteen cents net profit for every dollar of sales.

General and admin expenses usually remain constant over a short term of about one year. Also, from our discussion of GP Ratio, we know that certain direct cost components remain constant over a range of production levels.

Therefore, the net profit increases at a higher rate for any increase in revenue and vice versa.

iii) Asset Turnover Ratio

Asset turnover ratio is the efficiency of employing the company's asset base in producing sales revenue. A higher ratio indicates more efficient use of the company's assets—Exhibit 7.4.

Ratio / Year	2014	2013	Formula
Asset turnover ratio	1.47	1.54	= Sales / Average total assets
Where			
Sales =	2,163,545	2,084,534	Values from 'Model Profit & Loss a/c' (Chapter III)
Total Assets -year beginning (a)	1,393,445	1,313,524	Values from 'Model Balance Sheet' (Chapter II)
Total Assets -year end (b)	1,542,515	1,393,445	
Average Total Assets c = (a+b)/2	1,467,980	1,353,485	Arithmatical calculation
		Exhibit 7.4	

Model Company		
Balance Sheet as at 31 Dec 2014		
(Summary form)		
Description	2014	2013
ASSETS		
Non-current assets	671,193	649,006
Current assets	871,322	744,439
Total assets	1,542,515	1,393,445
EQUITY & LIABILITIES		
Total equity	739,729	694,042
Non-current liabilities	345,000	255,000
Current liabilities	457,786	444,403
Total equity & liabilities	1,542,515	1,393,445

2 Average Assets = 1,467,980

1

Exhibit 7.5

We take 'Total assets' as of 31 Dec 2013 and 31 Dec 2014 from the Balance Sheet (Exhibit 7.5, marked 1) to calculate 'average assets' (marked 2.)

We compute the average of total assets employed in the company during the year, as we relate this value to the revenue earned during the year.

The Asset Turnover ratio is computed by relating the revenue (turnover) from Profit & Loss Account (Exhibit 7.6, marked 3) to the average assets.

Model Company

Profit and Loss Account for the year ended 31 Dec 2014
(Summary form)

Description	2014	2013
Revenue	2,163,545	2,084,534
LESS Direct cost	(1,422,992)	(1,353,320)
Gross profit	740,553	731,214
ADD Other Income	45,000	50,000
LESS General & Admin Cost	(442,317)	(424,311)
Operating Profit	343,237	356,903
LESS Interest on loans	(17,550)	(15,750)
Net Profit before Taxes	325,687	341,153
LESS Taxes	(30,000)	(32,000)
Net Profit	295,687	309,153

Revenue for year 2014

Exhibit 7.6

Asset turnover ratio of 1.47 means that the company makes $1.47 in revenue for every dollar invested in assets.

Revenue per Employee

For a law firm or a company in a consulting business, we can compute *revenue per employee* as a *substitute for the Asset Turnover Ratio*. What matters is the billed amount for a consulting company vs. the number of lawyers or consultants employed.

Revenue per employee = Net revenue / no. of employees

Identify a trend

You can analyze the trend by comparing the ratios of the same company for five consecutive years.

Peer comparison

Compare these ratios with that of the company's competitor. It will show if the financial performance needs improvement.

You can compare the company's assets turnover ratio with that of the competitor subject to one condition. The *aging of assets* and the *technology* used by both companies should be similar. Aging and technology have a significant impact on assets value and productivity, and hence when these factors are not identical, you cannot use the asset turnover ratios for comparison.

∞

2. Working Capital Management Ratios

Current assets less current liabilities is the working capital.

We can monitor and control the working capital components, viz., Accounts Receivable, Accounts Payable, and Inventory using the turnover ratios.

i) Accounts Receivable Turnover Ratio

The Accounts Receivable Turnover ratio provides a measure of the *customer follow-up* in collecting outstanding amounts.

We need two values to compute the ratio — customers' balances and credit sales during the year.

Customer outstanding may not be available directly from the Balance Sheet. The same is grouped along with other similar receivables to show one value under the heading 'Trade & Other Receivables.' Below (Exhibit 7.7) is the break-up of Trade & Other Receivables from our model Balance Sheet.

Trade & Other Receivables			
Description	2014	2013	Remarks
Accounts Receivable	180,300	173,710	
Prepaid expenses	101,000	78,400	
Refundable deposits	80,400	51,300	
Others	40,155	7,469	
TOTAL: Trade and other receivables	401,855	310,879	Values from 'Model Balance Sheet' (Chapter II)
		Exhibit 7.7	

Please also refer to the next exhibit for the *business process* related to credit sales and the resulting customer outstanding balance.

The focus is on customer outstanding; how to monitor and control the same. Exhibit 7.8 explains the ratio and its formula.

Accounts Receivable Turnover ratio			
Ratio /Year	2014	2013	Formula
Accounts Receivable Turnover ratio	12.22	11.62	= Sales/ Average receivables
Where			
Sales =	2,163,545	2,084,534	
Receivable -year beginning (a)	173,710	185,000	
Receivable -year end (b)	180,300	173,710	
Average receivables c = (a+b)/2	177,005	179,355	Arithmatical calculation
		Exhibit 7.8	

Good credit policy, efficient collection department, and good customer base yield higher Accounts Receivable Turnover Ratio.

A lower ratio may indicate an inadequate demand for the company's products or the sales department extending a longer credit period to its customers.

Besides, the sales strategy of attracting new customers by extending a higher credit period to beat the competition can be the reason for a lower Accounts Receivable Turnover Ratio.

ii) Accounts Payable Turnover Ratio

The focus is on vendor outstanding resulting from credit purchase as shown below:

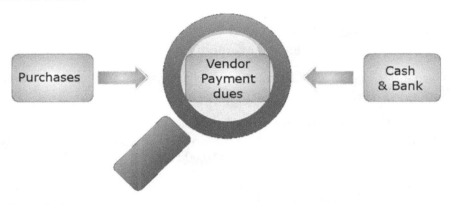

The ratio is:

Ratio /Year	2014	2013	Formula
Accounts Payable Turnover ratio	6.00	6.20	= Total purchases / Average payables

Payable turnover ratio six means the company pays its suppliers in two months from the purchase date. Twelve-month purchase values are used to compute the ratio, and hence twelve divided by six (12/6 = 2) gives the number of months vendor dues that are outstanding.

Higher is the ratio; shorter is the time suppliers are paid.

The manager has to look at the accounts payable turnover ratio to know if the company is paying its suppliers in time.

You can compare the company's ratio with its competitor to know if there is scope to negotiate better credit terms with its suppliers.

iii) Inventory Turnover Ratio

The formula for the inventory ratio is:

Inventory Turnover = Cost of Goods Sold/ Average Inventory

The cost of goods sold is the direct cost of goods sold: material costs + production labor + production overhead.

The ratio gives how many times in Dollar terms the inventory is sold during the year.

For example, COGS is sixty-thousand dollars, and the average inventory carried by the company is ten-thousand dollars, then the inventory turnover ratio is $60,000 divided by $10,000 = 6.

It means the company turns over six times its inventory over twelve months. Alternatively, the company holds two months of its COGS value as inventory.

You compute the average inventory as the average of the year beginning and year-end values.

Comparing this ratio with the previous year or a competitor provides valuable information if it is doing better in its inventory management.

Take care when calculating average inventory in the case of a seasonal business. If the high season falls in the middle of the year, you may apply the monthly average and the monthly average COGS for computing the inventory turnover ratio.

A higher inventory ratio shows efficient inventory management.

∞

3. Liquidity Ratios

Liquidity refers to the ability of a company to meet short-term financial commitments on time.

Take necessary care to manage the company's liquidity. Maintaining adequate liquidity is incredibly important for a company's reputation and business continuity.

Ratio analysis of current assets and current liabilities from the Balance Sheet is a good measure of a company's liquidity.

The current ratio and **quick ratio** are the two liquidity ratios.

i) Current Ratio

It is the ratio of current assets to current liabilities.

Ratio / Year	2014	2013	Formula
Current ratio	1.90	1.68	=current assets / current liabilities
Where			
Current Assets	871,322	744,439	Values from 'Model Balance Sheet' (Chapter II)
Current Liabilities	457,786	444,403	

Cash, bank deposits, receivables from customers, and inventory are the current assets.

Payables to vendors and short-term debts are the current liabilities.

Please refer to the topics Assets (page no.12) and Outside Liabilities (page no. 18) under Chapter 2 Balance Sheet for a discussion on current assets and current liabilities.

The current ratio of 1.9 means the company's current assets are 1.9 times its current liabilities.

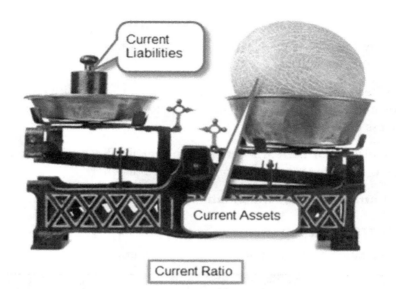

Current Ratio

The current ratio of *'two'* is considered ideal. However, as with other ratios, this value can be different for different industries. Analyze current ratio along with quick ratio to study the liquidity risk.

ii) Quick Ratio

Please refer to the below Exhibit for the quick ratio formula and example:

Ratio / Year	2014	2013	Formula
Quick ratio	1.14	0.94	=quick assets / current liabilities
Where			
Quick Assets = Current Assets - Inventory	520,334	419,028	Values from 'Model Balance Sheet' (Chapter II)
Current Liabilities	457,786	444,403	

Quick assets = Current assets - Inventory.

Quick assets (quickly convertible assets) represent that portion of current assets that the company can convert into cash in the normal course of business in a defined period.

For example, customers with 30 days credit terms means the company can expect to convert the customer balance into cash in 30 days from the date of sales.

However, the conversion of inventory into cash depends on production, storage, and sales. Thus, raw material inventory to cash conversion takes a longer time. Hence, we exclude inventory while computing the quick assets.

A quick ratio of 1.14 means the company's quick assets are 1.14 times of short-term financial obligations.

Important: As a general rule of thumb, a quick ratio of less than one is an indicator of liquidity risk.

How to Improve and Maintain Liquidity

Ensure you have the right capital structure—particularly during the *startup, expansion, and rapid growth* phases.

If your company is in one of the above phases, you need to pay special care on the present and the projected liquidity.

Remember, inadequate liquidity is risky for business continuity, while excess liquidity comes with an additional cost, thus reducing the company's profitability.

∞

4. Return on Capital Employed

ROCE = Earnings before Interest and Tax (EBIT) / Average Capital Employed

Capital employed means equity plus long-term debt. This ratio shows the efficiency of money invested to generate income.

You can use ROCE to compare the profitability of two or more companies in the same industry.

∞

5. Key Points in Ratio Analysis

i) Importance of Ratio Formula

Please note to read the ratio formulae when you do a ratio analysis, as there are no standard formulae for some ratios.

Example:

Inventory Turnover Ratio= Cost of Goods Sold/ Average Inventory

Alternate formula used

Inventory Turnover Ratio = Sales / Inventory

ii) Related Ratios

Avoid forming an opinion by looking at one or two ratios in isolation. Look at all related ratios together.

Example: Ratios for profitability

GP ratio,

NP ratio, and

Asset turnover ratio.

GP & NP Ratios alone will not provide a correct sign of profitability. Analyze profitability using GP & NP Ratios with Asset Turnover Ratio.

Irrespective of good GP & NP Ratios, a low Asset Turnover Ratio may signify that the company is not using its assets to its full potential.

iii) Business Model, Strategy, and Financial Ratios

Understand the business strategy and analyze the ratios to form an opinion on the financial status of a company.

Please refer to the topic Business Perspective (page no.52) under Chapter 5 Demystify Financial Statements.

∞

Chapter Recap

When we know the relationships between values in financial statements, we can derive valuable insight into those values using mathematical ratios.

We have discussed Profitability Ratios, Working Capital Management Ratios, Liquidity Ratios, Return on Capital Employed (ROCE), and the key points we should consider in ratio analysis.

The insight gained from ratio analysis in the backdrop of the overall business perspective helps managers make prudent financial decisions and maximize wealth creation.

∞

In the last three chapters, we have learned how to read and interpret financial statements. In the next three chapters, we will learn planning & control in financial management.

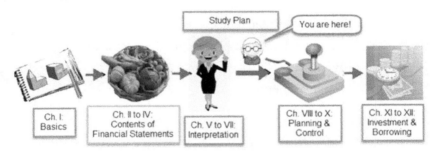

∞∞

CHAPTER 8

Working Capital Management

Welcome to the Planning & Control arena in Finance!

In this chapter, we will cover working capital management, which is an *everyday financial control* measure. Working Capital Management keeps your company financially fit.

Working capital is the net funds used for current assets & current liabilities where

Current assets are:

- ✓ Cash & Bank balances,
- ✓ Customer balances (Accounts Receivables),
- ✓ Inventory,
- ✓ Prepaid expenses, and

Current liabilities are:

- ✓ Expenses payable,
- ✓ Supplier balances (Accounts Payables),
- ✓ Short-term borrowing, and
- ✓ The short-term portion of long-term borrowing.

Business model and business strategy play a role in determining the size of the working capital. Business strategy determines the purchase and sales credit periods. Sales strategy, market dynamics, and production technology employed determine inventory level.

Efficient working capital management is crucial for effective financial performance.

Chapter Contents

1. Why Is Working Capital Management Crucial?
2. Managing Working Capital
3. Working Capital Cycle
4. Working Capital for a Growing Business

∞

1. Why Is Working Capital Management Crucial?

Effective management of funds employed in day-to-day operations is an inseparable part of overall financial management. Inefficient working capital management would cause financial and reputation loss for the company.

Let's now understand what happens with inadequate working capital management in specific scenarios.

i) Customer Outstanding

Poor management of customer outstanding results in loss because of an increase in

Bad debts, and

Cost of funds locked in higher outstanding balances.

ii) Vendor Payments

A company will suffer reputation loss if it delays the payment to its suppliers. Trying to reduce the interest costs by delaying supplier payments can be detrimental to the company's image.

iii) Inventory Control

Inadequate attention to keeping the inventory at optimum levels can cause loss due to interruptions in production because of non-availability of material in time and wastage because of obsolescence, rusting, etc.

∞

2. Managing Working Capital

You can highlight where the working capital management is sub-optimal using Ratio Analysis and exercise control by drafting and enforcing policies and procedures.

i) Ratio Analysis

Financial ratios highlight whether the working capital is at its optimum size or not compared to business volume. To recap, please refer to our discussion on the topic 'Working Capital Management Ratios' (page no. 70) under Chapter 7 Ratio Analysis.

ii) Policies and Procedures

Define policies & guidelines for each segment of WC management and fix responsibility to report on exceptions.

a) Customer Outstanding

A Company allows its customers one month from the day of sales to pay. The accounts division responsible for collecting the customer dues should report to the unit manager when there is a payment delay beyond the credit period.

For instances of customer outstanding beyond, say, two months, the credit policy mandates an action such as 'stop sales and start recovery proceedings.'

Vital elements of Accounts Receivables management are:

- ✓ Fixing credit period for sales based on the business model, strategy, and market dynamics;
- ✓ Implementing a procedure to approve customers who are eligible for credit period;
- ✓ Fixing limits on credit amount and credit period for individual customers; and
- ✓ Monitoring and reporting on collections.

b) Vendor Dues

Negotiate with suppliers for credit purchases instead of cash purchases. A good reputation helps the company to get favorable credit terms. Keeping track of payable balances & due dates is made easy using present-day Accounting & ERP systems. Cash flow planning can ensure the availability of funds for meeting supplier payments in time.

c) Inventory

Inventory needs special mention.

Inventory includes:

- Raw materials,
- Semi-finished goods,
- Finished goods, and
- Consumables.

Inventory management measures are:

- ✓ Implementing minimum order quantity, re-orders level, and economic order quantity;
- ✓ Fixing reporting responsibilities for aging and obsolete stock;
- ✓ Taking adequate measures to prevent pilferage, such as periodic stocktaking and reconciliation with book-keeping records.

Inventory management requires adequate management attention. ERP programs help a great deal in implementing modern inventory management techniques.

Inventory management is a topic that has its depth and complexity. Companies entrust inventory management responsibilities to persons having specialized knowledge and experience in materials management.

∞

3. Working Capital Cycle

Working capital is funded by

> Supplier credit,
>
> Short-term borrowing, and
>
> Long-term funds—equity & term loans.

and used in

> Customer outstanding,
>
> Inventory, and
>
> Cash for operations.

Banks lend money to a company as overdraft, cash credits, invoice discounting, trust receipts, etc. These short-term facilities are for financing working capital. We'll cover more on the borrowing under Chapter 12, 'How to Borrow from Banks.'

Financial prudence requires that companies use long-term funding to finance inventory.

A simple working capital cycle is as in the picture next:

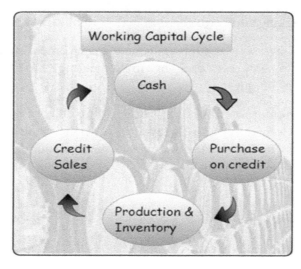

∞

4. Working Capital for a Growing Business

Is your business on a rapid growth path?

During the company's rapid growth phase, inventory level increases exponentially. The company needs additional stock to meet the estimated increase in future sales. As we know, there is a lead-time in ordering, receiving, and completing the production and keeping the finished goods ready to meet the customer demand.

Again, prudent financial planning requires long-term funds for financing inventory. Therefore, you have to forecast the required stock and arrange long-term funding under this scenario.

I recommend you take the help of finance professionals to make sales and inventory projections and plan the needed funding during your company's high sales growth phase.

∞

Chapter Recap

The current assets and current liabilities of a company make up its working capital. Working capital management refers to day-to-day *financial control* exercise. It requires an understanding of the working capital cycle for the business.

You can implement policies and procedures and exercise sound working capital management that highlights exceptions.

Working capital management is crucial for sustaining the financial success of a company.

∞

We understand the day-to-day financial control measures. In the next chapter, we will learn budgeting.

∞∞∞

CHAPTER 9

Budgeting

Setting goals is the first step in turning the invisible into the visible.

- Tony Robbins

∞

Where do you want your company one year from now? The answer probably lies in your company's budget!

A budget is a planning document to achieve the company's goal, aligned with the corporate mission, usually covering one financial year.

A budget is a business roadmap. It tells the stakeholders within the company what they need to achieve.

The budget elucidates targeted sales, production, purchases, and overheads; quantifies required resources to achieve the targets.

You can use budgeting both for profit-seeking and not profit-seeking organizations.

Chapter Contents

1. How Does a Company Benefit from the Budget?
2. Essentials of a Good Budget
3. Success in Budgeting
4. Budgeting Approaches
5. Types of Budget
6. The Budgeting Process
7. Who Makes the Budget?
8. Budget Approval

∞

1. How Does a Company Benefit from the Budget?

i) Budget Sets the Tone for Future Performance

The budget acts as a guiding document for the management to follow and achieve the company's goal, leading to overall corporate performance and growth.

Usually, it is prepared and approved in advance for one financial year.

The budget sets the targeted financial performance along with relevant quantitative data.

ii) Budget for Performance Evaluation and Control

The budget acts as a benchmark for performance monitoring and control.

The budget, when approved, gives direction to all levels of management.

The budget vs. actual format of the MIS reports provides a significant insight into current performance. Please refer to the topic, Comparison with Budget (page no. 55) under Chapter 6 Monitoring Financial Performance.

iii) Budget as a Tool for Effective Delegation

Delegation involves assigning tasks, fixing responsibility, and the authority necessary to complete the tasks, from one level to the next level down the corporate hierarchy.

Budget facilitates delegation at all managerial levels. Defining the tasks and fixing targets keeping the budget as a guideline becomes easier.

Budget-based targets are fixed when the top management approves the budget. Then it is the managerial duty to assign responsibility & provide the required authority to achieve the budgeted targets.

∞

2. Essentials of a Good Budget

Budget should be

- ✓ Achievable as well as challenging;
- ✓ Beware of and address the competition;
- ✓ Reflecting interrelationships between costs and revenues;
- ✓ Exploiting opportunities;
- ✓ Beware of technological obsolescence and advent of new technologies; and
- ✓ Exploring and exploiting core competencies and strengths.

∞

3. Success in Budgeting

Top Management Commitment

Budgeting needs top management's commitment and operations management's dedication.

Knowledge of the Company

Successful budgeting requires knowledge of the company.

Thus, the budgeting exercise needs:

- ✓ Clarity on the company goals;
- ✓ A clear understanding of market dynamics and constraints in which the company operates; and
- ✓ Knowledge of needed resources.

Do a reality check, seek to understand your organization inside out. Then, you are ready to go for and reap the benefits of budgeting.

Realistic Assumptions

Budgeting is a future-oriented exercise. Therefore, you need to make estimates based on specific assumptions. The assumptions for a budget may be:

- ✓ Effect of competition on sales,
- ✓ Availability of raw materials,
- ✓ Technological changes,
- ✓ Rate of foreign exchange,
- ✓ Economic trends.

You can add your own, apart from the above. The budget document should clearly state the assumptions based on which the budget was prepared.

Assumptions enable:

- ✓ Budget evaluation,
- ✓ Users of the budget understand it better, and
- ✓ Explain budget vs. actual variance.

∞

4. Budgeting Approaches

Top-down, bottom-up, and mixed approaches are the three approaches to budgeting.

i) Top-down Approach

Top management fixes targets and goals, distributed down to divisions and departments—for the operational management to achieve.

ii) Bottom-up Approach

Operational management for their respective responsibility areas fixes budget quantities and values.

In consultation with the operational management, the budget coordinator consolidates the budget values upwards in the corporate hierarchy to arrive at the company's master budget.

iii) Mixed Approach

Generally, companies use both the top-down and the bottom-up approaches. Top management sets overall corporate goals and policies, and operational management fixing actionable department level targets consolidated upwards, arriving at the corporate objectives set by top management.

5. Types of Budget

The budget types are:

i) Fixed or Static budget,

ii) Flexible budget,

iii) Continuous or Rolling Budget, and

iv) Zero-based budgeting

i) Fixed or Static Budget

A fixed budget is a budget for **one activity level** (page no. 5.) A fixed budget is suitable for departmental budgets such as Admin and HR, where cost remains the same irrespective of changes in the activity level.

A company may prepare the entire budget as fixed when operating in a stable production and sales environment.

ii) Flexible Budget

The budget prepared for a **range of activity levels** is the flexible budget. A flexible budget is a budget prepared for:

✓ Optimistic level,
✓ Pessimistic level, and
✓ Expected or best guess estimate level.

The optimistic level approach is the best-case scenario budget; the opposite would be the pessimistic approach.

The expected or best guess estimate is a balanced level budget, via media between the optimistic & pessimistic levels.

You can adjust the flexible budget to the activity level achieved by comparing it with the actual performance.

iii) Continuous or Rolling Budget

The budget is customarily prepared for twelve months—covering the financial year. You prepare and add the thirteenth-month budget when the first month's budget period is over. Thus, a twelve-month budget is available throughout the financial year in a rolling budget.

Illustration: Consider the budget from Jan 2014 to Dec 2014. End of Jan 2014, you add the budget for Jan 2015. This is a rolling budget.

The disadvantage of the rolling budget

In this model, the company does the budgeting exercise every month. Budget managers take it easy as budgeting becomes a routine task carried out every month. Therefore, the quality of the budget suffers.

Companies adopt a three-month rolling budget instead of a monthly rolling budget to mitigate this disadvantage.

iv) Zero Based Budgeting

Zero-based budgeting takes an entirely **fresh look at each item in the budget**. Every claim for a budget expense should be evaluated and justified.

You would have noticed the key difference in this approach. The budget is **not prepared** by taking the previous year's actual values as a reference point.

Zero-based budgeting is a time-consuming exercise because the managers have to evaluate every budget item exhaustively before accepting them.

To mitigate this difficulty, companies may implement zero-based budgeting **once every three years**.

∞

6. The Budgeting Process

Co-ordination & Deliberation

Budgeting is a centrally coordinated, corporate-wide exercise. The budgeting team comprising the senior managers should deliberate market conditions, available resources, and targets.

Budget Preparation

Companies prepare the budget by taking either the previous year's budget or actual values as a reference point and adjust them for current market conditions while meeting the long-term organizational goals.

Business Activities to be budgeted

Budget is prepared for each of the following activities:

Sales,

Production,

Purchase,

Maintenance,

Marketing,

Admin & general expenses,

Profit and loss, and

Cash flow.

Operating Constraints

Operating constraint is a limiting factor.

It puts a limit on the company's business activity. The operating constraints are unique to specific industries.

We can understand the operating constraint with narration.

For some companies, production is the limiting factor because of government regulations on the supply of raw materials, pollution control, or the availability of a skilled workforce. In such a scenario, the production budget is prepared first, addressing the constraints. For other companies, the sales budget is prepared first.

Identification of the *operating constraint* in which the company operates is a crucial first step to budgeting.

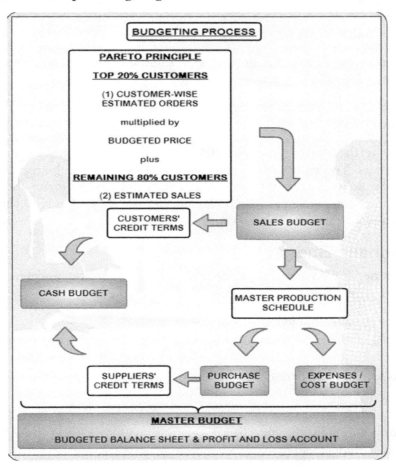

Sales Budget

The budget is prepared based on quantity, where it is measurable. Where quantity is not measurable or not relevant, the budget is prepared for sales in dollar terms.

For example, budgets for grocery stores and consultancy businesses are prepared for sales in amounts.

Projected sales quantity multiplied by the budgeted selling price gives the revenue budget.

Applying the Pareto principle, 80% of the sales are from 20% of the customers. You compute the projected sales quantity for the top 20% of the customers. Later, for the remaining customers, estimate the sales quantities. Then calculate the budgeted sales revenue by multiplying the sales quantity and the budgeted price.

Purchase Budget

Quantities for opening stock, desired closing stock, and budgeted sales determine *purchase quantity*.

We know (quantitatively),

$$Opening\ stock\ +\ purchases\ -\ sales\ =\ closing\ stock$$

Therefore, we can derive (quantitatively),

$$Purchases\ =\ desired\ closing\ stock\ +\ budgeted\ sales\ -\ opening\ stock$$

Multiplication of the purchased quantity with budgeted price gives purchase budget value.

Apply the above computation for 20% of the materials, which is 80% of the purchases in values. You can estimate the remaining 80% of the materials, based on the company's experience, adjusting for the expected changes in price.

Add to the value of the purchases computed as above—estimated shipping, insurance, and transportation costs to compute the purchases budget.

General and Admin Expenses Budget

General and admin overhead cost budget is prepared with the previous year's budget or actual values, adjusting for the cost escalation.

Also, contracts such as for office rental, manpower supply provide a basis for a portion of the overhead cost budget.

Budgeted Cash Flow

Reflecting the cash effects of all the budgeted transactions is the cash flow budget. Thus, you prepare the budgeted cash flow by referring to:

- ✓ Sales and credit terms,
- ✓ Purchase and credit terms,
- ✓ Repairs & maintenance, and
- ✓ Prepaid and accrued expenses.

The accounts department makes the cash budget.

∞

7. Who Makes the Budget?

Preparation and submission of the budget figures within the general guidelines laid by the top management is the responsibility of the company's department heads.

Example: Sales Department makes the sales budget. The maintenance department submits a budget for repairs and maintenance costs. The Admin or the Accounts department prepares the budget for General and Admin Expenses.

Preparation of Cash budget is the responsibility of the Accounts & Finance Department.

The Master Budget

The Accounts and Finance department has a crucial responsibility in rolling out the master budget. Usually, the CFO acts as the **budget coordinator** with responsibilities for master budget compilation.

∞

8. Budget Approval

Top management approves the draft budget. The budget coordinator circulates the approved budget to the department heads.

Top management approves the budget before the beginning of the budgeted year.

∞

Chapter Recap

Budgeting exercise involves participation by all management levels. The budget sets the direction, facilitates delegation, and acts as the performance evaluation tool in an organization.

Companies prepare the budget, beginning with targets fixed by top management and breaking down the targets into actionable operational goals by middle and lower managerial personnel.

A systematic approach beginning with a sales budget to a cash budget and a master budget ensures a company implements budgeting.

Adequate attention and care while making assumptions is a prerequisite for the best results of a budgeting exercise.

∞

In the next chapter, we will learn the tools for making short-term financial decisions. Continue reading.

∞∞∞

CHAPTER 10

Break-Even Analysis for Key Financial Decisions

I can't change the direction of the wind, but I can adjust my sails always to reach my destination -Jimmy Dean

∞

If you were associated with a startup business venture, you would have faced this question from your well-wishers:

Are you breaking even?

At break-even, revenue equals the costs incurred to generate that revenue. It is that point of a company's growth curve when the business stops incurring loss and earns a profit.

Thus, the break-even point is the no-loss-no-profit sales quantity or the sales amount

Break-even analysis is an indispensable tool for ***short-term*** decision-making not only for startups but also for running businesses.

Using the break-even analysis, we can build economic models for a single product or a business. Models help us identify the most financially beneficial decision. The resources are committed, not by chance but by choice.

All types of companies—manufacturing, trading & rendering services can apply break-even analysis models for decision-making.

Chapter Contents

∞

1. Cost Behavior — Variable and Fixed Costs

The Break-even analysis is based on the cost classification into **variable and fixed** costs.

i) Variable Costs

We know that expenses vary depending on the activity or production level. A company can achieve higher production, incurring higher costs.

Costs that increase with an increase in activity (production or sales) are variable.

Examples of variable costs:

- ✓ Materials,
- ✓ The labor cost associated with production,
- ✓ Commission paid to salespeople,
- ✓ Shipping cost.

ii) Fixed Costs

Fixed costs are the expenses or costs that remain constant irrespective of changes in the activity level.

Examples of fixed costs:

- ✓ Rent
- ✓ Supervisor and admin staff salaries
- ✓ Electricity for lighting.

You will appreciate the importance of cost classification into variable and fixed when we go through a simple break-even analysis model.

2. Break-Even Analysis Model

Consider you are making and selling pencil boxes in your spare time (Exhibit 10.1.)

Break-even Analysis model	
Wood & carbide cost per box	$5.00
Hired part time carpenter	$3.00
Your variable cost is	$8.00
Your selling price per box	$10.00
Selling price minus variable cost is called contribution margin.	
Contribution margin per box	$2.00
You have rented a small garage for the purpose.	
Monthly rent	$100.00
This is your fixed cost.	
Break even sales (no. of boxes)	=fixed cost/ contribution margin
You need to sell 50 boxes ($100/ $2) to break even.	
Break even sales in Dollars	=Break even sales (no. of boxes) x selling price
Your break even sales is $500 (50 boxes x $10).	
	Exhibit 10.1

To recover your rent, you need to sell fifty boxes. It is the break-even sales quantity. The Break-even sales amount is five hundred dollars.

Any sales above fifty numbers will bring you a profit of two dollars a box.

Break-even Analysis Equation

The relationship between sales, cost, and profit is:

$$\text{Sales} - \text{variable cost} - \text{fixed cost} = \text{Profit}$$

Cost classification as variable and fixed is the basis for break-even analysis.

∞

3. Break-even Analysis—Scalable Model

The real-life situation is never as simple as we saw in our previous break-even analysis model. The next model depicts how we can use the concept in a larger operation.

Consider you are running a workshop producing a machine. Exhibit 10.2 depicts the scaled-up break-even model.

Break-even analysis scaled up model

You have computed your variable cost for making 5 machines as:

Direct material	26,300
Direct labor	5,450
General maintenance	750
Sales commission	500
Total variable cost	**33,000**

Your fixed commitment is

Building rent	10,000
Property tax	3,000
Electricity & water charges	500
Telephone	700
Depreciation	2,500
Insurance	300
Advertising	2,000
General office salaries	7,000
General maintenance	1,000
Total fixed cost	**27,000**

Variable cost to produce 5 machines	33,000
Variable cost for one machine	6,600

Consider you can sell your machine for $9,300

Your contribution margin per machine is $2,700 (selling price $9,300 minus variable cost per machine $6,600).

No. of machines you break even is 10 (fixed cost $27,000 /contribution margin $2,700)

Break even sales in Dollars is $93,000 (break even sales -no. of machines, 10 x price $9,300)

Exhibit 10.2

You might have noticed that general maintenance appears in both variable and fixed costs. It is because a portion of this cost is variable.

∞

4. Multiple Products Scenario

It is most often the case that a company sells multiple products. You can apply the break-even analysis in a multi-product scenario with additional computations.

Get the following computations:

- ✓ Sales mix,
- ✓ Weighted average selling price, *and*
- ✓ Weighted average variable cost.

The formula for computing the weighted average selling price is:

(the price of product_1 x sales percentage of product_1) + (the price of product_2 x sales percentage of product_2) and so on.

Calculate weighted average variable cost the same way.

The next step is computing the contribution margin for the sales mix.

Contribution margin = Weighted average selling price - weighted average variable cost.

The final step is computing the break-even sales for the sales mix.

Break-even sales = Fixed cost /Contribution Margin.

Refer to Exhibits 10.3 & 10.4 for a sales mix with a three-product break-even analysis model.

Consider you have 3 products, their sales percentages, prices & the respective computed variable costs per unit as under:

	Sales percentage	Price	Variable cost
Product 1	30%	$300	$250
Product 2	25%	$500	$400
Product 3	45%	$700	$500
Total	100%		

Your fixed cost is say, $100,000.

Weighted average price = Product 1 (price x sales percentage) + product 2 (price x sales percentage) + product 3 (price x sales percentage)

$$=(\$300 \times 30\% + \$500 \times 25\% + \$700 \times 45\%)$$

$$= \$530$$

Weighted average variable cost = Product 1 (variable cost x percentage) + product 2 (variable cost x percentage) + product 3 (variable cost x percentage)

$$=(\$250 \times 30\% + \$400 \times 25\% + \$500 \times 45\%)$$

$$=\$400$$

Weighted average contribution margin = weighted average price minus weighted average cost

$$=\$130$$

Break even sales in no. of pieces = fixed cost / contribution margin

$$=770 \text{ pieces}$$

Break even sales in Dollars = break even sales in numbers x weighted average price

$$=\$408,100$$

...Continued in next picture

Exhibit 10.3

Continued from previous picture…	
Product-wise break even sales in units	
Product 1	231
Product 2	193
Product 3	347
Total	771
(Difference of 1 number is due to rounding off as we can not have fraction of a product)	
Product-wise break even sales in Dollars	
Product 1	$69,300
Product 2	$96,500
Product 3	$242,900
Total	$408,700
(Difference between the two values $408,100 vs. $408,700 is due to rounding off)	

Exhibit 10.4

You may create as many models to represent as many sales mix.

∞

5. How do you Use Break-Even Analysis?

Having understood the concept, let us dive into how a manager can use break-even analysis in his decision-making role.

Break-Even models help you decide the selling price:

> i) In a product launch, and
>
> ii) In special pricing scenarios such as a competitive market, special order, off-season, or a promotion.

i) Product Launch

In a product launch, there is a gestation period. It is the period for the product to gain acceptance in the market, recover cost and start making a profit.

Break-even analysis is a handy tool for managers to estimate the length of the gestation period before the product starts making a profit. Thus, the managers can plan the funding required for a product launch.

ii) Special Pricing Scenarios

A product's price is computed as the sum of Total Cost and Profit Margin (Total Cost = Fixed Cost + Variable Cost.)

However, situations may warrant a discounted price for your products. You may want to set a product's price at less than its total cost. Cost behavior analysis provides necessary information about the minimum price to cover the variable cost. You can build a new break-even model for a discounted price. The new model helps to estimate the potential loss.

∞

6. What Care should you take to Use Break-Even Models?

Break-even analysis models are valid for i) the relevant range and ii) the short-term.

i) Relevant Range

Fixed costs remain fixed, subject to a narrow range of activity levels (page no. 5.) For example, if the production capacity of a factory with two shifts is five thousand units. If you need to increase the production beyond this level, three-shift working may be required. Increasing the number of shifts from two to three will increase the fixed costs such as the supervisor's salary and utility costs.

The break-even model built for two-shift working has a relevant range with an upper production limit of five thousand units in the above example.

ii) Short-term

Fixed costs remain fixed for a short-term only, say one year. In the long-term, *all expenses vary* — increase in rent, property tax, and salary. So, the break-even analysis model is *valid only for the short term.*

Do remember and insist the above two limiting factors, viz., relevant range, and short term, are mentioned clearly in any break-even models presented to the management *to avoid costly mistakes.*

∞

7. Decision Making using Break-Even Analysis Models

Break-even analysis provides you with indispensable fundamental financial information and a starting point in your decision-making.

Break-even analysis is only a piece of financial information.

Your business acumen, gained through your study of the market, experience with your product portfolio, future prospects, technology changes, strategies, and strength of your competitors, your core competence play a role while taking a decision.

∞

Chapter Recap

Break-even analysis is a tool based on cost behavior for

- ✓ Short-term decision-making, and
- ✓ Within the relevant range.

You can build sales-cost-profit models to study different scenarios before committing resources.

Break-Even models help you decide the selling price:

i) In a product launch, and

ii) In special pricing scenarios such as a competitive market, special order, off-season, or a promotion.

∞

In the next chapter, we will learn capital expenditure evaluation techniques.

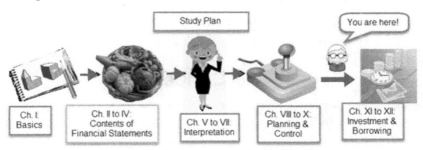

oooo

CHAPTER 11

Capital Expenditure Budgeting

Capital expenditure budgeting refers to non-current assets procurement plan. Non-current assets are assets such as building, plant & machinery needed to produce goods.

We discussed operating expenditure (opex) budgeting under Chapter 9. In this chapter, we will discuss capital expenditure (capex) budgeting.

Chapter Contents

1. The Concept
2. Terms and Methodologies
2. Capex Evaluation Techniques
3. Important Note on Capex Evaluation

1. The Concept

Your company needs to incur capex to expand its business by adding new products or by increasing the production capacity for the existing products.

Often, the company has to choose a project out of different options using the capex evaluation techniques.

The capex evaluation technique is a financial tool to *evaluate and choose one capex option out of competing projects* that maximize wealth.

Capex evaluation techniques use *net cash flows* and *discount rates* to compute the net gain or loss for an investment option. We compare the net gain or loss of the competing investment options to choose the best one.

We use *cash flows and not the 'net profit or net loss' concepts* in the capex evaluation techniques.

2. Terms and Methodologies

Let's learn the terms and methodologies in the capex evaluation techniques.

They are

> i) Cash Flows,
>
> ii) Present Value, Future Value, and Discount Rate.
>
> iii) Mathematics behind PV, FV, and Discount Rate, and
>
> iv) FV & PV Tables.

i) Cash Flows

Cash flows consist of cash payments and cash receipts during the investment period.

Cash payments include cash outlay for the machinery & equipment purchases and for carrying on the business activity.

Cash receipts arise from the sale of goods and the sale of investment assets at the end of the investment period.

Let us consider an example:

Model Cash Flow	
Year	Cash flow
Year 0	(8,000)
Year 1	(250)
Year 2	2,500
Year 3	3,000
Year 4	3,750

Year 0: Purchase of machinery $8,000—cash out-flow,

Year 1: Receipts from sales $500, payments towards running cost $750—net cash out-flow $250,

Year 2: Receipts $3,500, payments $1,000—net cash in-flow $2,500,

Year 3: Receipts $4,000, payments $1,000—net cash in-flow $3,000, and

Year 4: Receipts machinery sales $4,000, payments towards effecting the machinery sales $250—net cash in-flow $3,750.

We tabulate the cash payments and receipts to summarize the investment cash flows as below:

ii) Present Value, Future Value, and Discount Rate

We know a specified amount of money today is not the equivalent of the same amount after one year. It is because of the **cost of capital** or, simply, **the interest**.

Consider one hundred dollars invested today in a Government bond to get one hundred and three dollars after one year on maturity. The difference amount of three dollars is the interest on the bond @ 3% per annum.

In other words, one hundred dollars is the **present value (PV)** for the one hundred and three dollars **future value (FV)** at a **discount rate** of three percent (r) for one year (n=1).

The discount rate is the cost of capital, the cost of procuring the funds for investment.

The example can be extrapolated—instead of one year, into five or ten years as required (n=5 or 10.)

iii) Mathematics behind PV, FV, and Discount Rate

If you are mathematically minded, please read this subtopic to understand the formula (*No harm if you skip!*)

First-year:

$$\$100 + (\$100 \times 3\%) = \$103$$

Therefore, adding 3% interest is the same as multiplying by 1.03. In a compound interest calculation, first-period interest is added to the principal to calculate the 2nd-period interest.

Second year:

$$\$103 \times 1.03 = \$106.09$$

Third year:

$$\$106.09 \times 1.03 = \$109.27$$

Rewriting the above,

$$\$100 \times 1.03 \times 1.03 \times 1.03 = \$109.27$$

Mathematical formula is:

$$PV \, (1+r)^n = FV$$

Where,

- ✓ PV = Present Value
- ✓ FV = Future Value
- ✓ r = Interest Rate (as a decimal value), and
- ✓ n = Number of Periods

Using the above formula, we can work out the Future Value FV when we know the Present Value PV, the Interest Rate r, and Number of Periods n.

Rearranging the above formula, we can find the Present Value when we know a Future Value, the Interest Rate, and the number of Periods.

$$PV = FV \, / \, (1+r)^n$$

The formula gives a present value for the expected or desired future value.

iv) Future Value and Present Value Tables

Do you want to bypass the formulae and computations described above? Use FV and PV tables.

You can refer to FV and PV tables with years on one side and the interest rate on the other side.

a) FV Table

The FV table shows how much one dollar today is worth at the end of a year in the future for an interest rate.

The tables (Exhibits 11.1 & 11.2) present ten years and four interest rate columns. You can Google and find full-length tables for more interest rates and year combinations.

Future Value table				
Years/Interest	3.00%	3.50%	4.00%	4.50%
1	1.03000	1.03500	1.04000	1.04500
2	1.06090	1.07123	1.08160	1.09203
3	1.09273	1.10872	1.12486	1.14117
4	1.12551	1.14752	1.16986	1.19252
5	1.15927	1.18769	1.21665	1.24618
6	1.19405	1.22926	1.26532	1.30226
7	1.22987	1.27228	1.31593	1.36086
8	1.26677	1.31681	1.36857	1.42210
9	1.30477	1.36290	1.42331	1.48610
10	1.34392	1.41060	1.48024	1.55297
		Exhibit 11.1		

b) PV Table

Consider you want to compute the present value for the desired future value of one hundred dollars in year 6 for an interest rate of four percent.

Refer to the Present Value table Exhibit 11.2 to get the desired PV factor.

> Year = 6
>
> Rate of Interest = 4%

Present value factor for $1 from the table $0.790315 (Highlighted in the table)

> Therefore, Present Value of $100 in year 6= 100 x 0.790315
>
> =$79.0315

Present Value of $1 to be Paid in Future			
Years	3.00%	3.50%	4.00%	4.50%
1	0.970874	0.966184	0.961538	0.956938
2	0.942596	0.933511	0.924556	0.915730
3	0.915142	0.901943	0.888996	0.876297
4	0.888487	0.871442	0.854804	0.838561
5	0.862609	0.841973	0.821927	0.802451
6	0.837484	0.813501	0.790315	0.767896
7	0.813092	0.785991	0.759918	0.734828
8	0.789409	0.759412	0.730690	0.703185
9	0.766417	0.733731	0.702587	0.672904
10	0.744094	0.708919	0.675564	0.643928
		Exhibit 11.2		

∞

3. Capex Evaluation Techniques

Having understood the terms used, let us learn the capital expenditure evaluation techniques:

> i) Payback Period,
>
> ii) Net Present Value, and
>
> iii) Internal Rate of Return.

i) Payback Period

It is the simplest method of weighing investment options.

The payback period is the number of years when the net cash generated from an investment equals the initial investment.

For example, consider the below investment cash flows:

Year 0:	$ -8,000
Year 1:	$ 1,500
Year 2:	$ 3,000
Year 3:	$ 3,500

In the example, cash out-flow is $8,000, the sum of cash inflows is $8,000, and the period is three years.

Thus, in three years, the cash generated from the investment equals the initial investment — the payback period of the investment is three years.

We compare the payback periods of different investment options and choose the one with the shortest payback period.

ii) Net Present Value

The net present value means the sum of the 'present values' of cash outflows and inflows.

In this method, first, we convert the investment cash flows into present values using the appropriate discount rates.

Then, we sum the present values to get the net 'present value' for each investment option.

Finally, we compare the net present values of the available investment options and choose the project with the highest NPV.

We can apply the NPV method when the initial cash outflows are equal for all the investments.

Example: Workings to Show NPV

Description	Cash flow (a)	PV factor @ 3% (b)	Present value (c = a x b)
Initial investment	(110,000)	1.00000	(110,000)
1st year	25,000	0.970874	24,272
2nd year	30,000	0.942596	28,278
3rd year	30,000	0.915142	27,454
4th year	32,000	0.888487	28,432
5th year	15,000	0.862609	12,939
Total			11,375
	Exhibit 11.3		

Exhibit 11.3:

> Column (a) gives the projected cash flows from the investment.
> Column (b) is the PV factor for the 3% discount rate, taken from the present value tables.
> Column (c) is the present values obtained by multiplying (a) & (b) values for the respective rows.

Thus the net present value for the investment is 11,375.

We compute the net present values for the remaining investment options, compare them and choose the option with the highest NPV.

Point to Consider — Discount Rate

Can we apply one discount rate for all the investment options to calculate NPV?

The answer is NO.

We can use different discount rates based on the risks associated with each investment option. The high-risk investment will carry a higher discount rate and vice versa.

Doing so will remove the risk imbalances between different investment options from the decision-making process.

iii) Internal Rate of Return

The internal rate of return is the discount rate when the sum of present values of all cash flows (both negative and positive) is equal to zero.

In this method, we compute the rate of return for the investment options and choose the one with the highest IRR.

Computing the IRR

Description	Cash flow (a)	PV factor @ 6.70% (b)	Present value (c = a x b)
Initial investment	(110,000)	1.00000	(110,000)
1st year	25,000	0.937207	23,430
2nd year	30,000	0.878357	26,351
3rd year	30,000	0.823203	24,696
4th year	32,000	0.771511	24,688
5th year	15,000	0.723066	10,846
Total			**11**

Exhibit 11.4

A higher discount rate decreases the sum of the present values and vice versa. This is because the 'present value' for the initial investment remains the same, and the 'present values' of cash inflows change as per higher or lower discount rates.

We arrive at a discount rate that gives the sum of present values equal to zero or a negligible amount by trial and error. By definition, this discount rate is the project's IRR.

In Exhibit 11.4, the IRR is 6.70% as it gives the sum of the present value of a negligible amount.

Higher than 6.7% would yield a significant negative value as the sum of the present value and vice versa.

We compute the IRR for the available investment options and compare them to choose the project with the highest IRR.

∞

4. Important Note on Capex Evaluation

I have covered the topic 'Capital Expenditure Budgeting' to familiarize you with the capex evaluation techniques.

You can now evaluate the options with your finance team, understanding their pros & cons.

Whenever you need to decide on CAPEX, I strongly recommend you to take advice from a professionally qualified finance person. He employs advanced finance models to evaluate and present the case, on which you can decide.

∞

Chapter Recap

Capital expenditure evaluation techniques provide a basis for choosing the right investment option that maximizes wealth from several available opportunities.

The CAPEX evaluation methods are:

1. Payback Period,
2. Net Present Value, and
3. Internal Rate of Return.

We use estimated future cash flows and discount rates in the CAPEX planning techniques.

It is advisable to take a finance professional's help while deciding on long-term investment options.

∞

You have learned the decision-making process that helps you choose a suitable investment. In the next chapter, you will learn how to borrow from banks.

Continue reading.

∞∞∞

CHAPTER 12

How to Borrow From Banks

Debt creates wealth only when you know how much debt is not too much.

∞

Borrowing money from banks and financial institutions is indispensable in most business models.

A loan can help the company meet a temporary shortfall in the cash flow or expand the business. In either case, the company should prepare a proposal to submit to the bank requesting the loan.

The company wants to borrow, and the banks operate to lend money. However, a successful loan application has to meet specific criteria for the banks to lend money. Let's learn that in this chapter.

Chapter Contents

1. Capital Employed
2. Capital Structure
3. Long-term Debt
4. What You Need to Get the Loan
5. EMI Mystery
6. Short Term Borrowing

∞

1. Capital Employed

Owners' equity and long-term debt make up the capital employed.

Owners' equity is the owners' money. In the Balance Sheet, capital and accumulated profits are the owners' equity.

Long-term debt is a loan with repayment obligations longer than one year.

As a general rule of thumb, capital employed should cover non-current assets and inventory costs.

2. Capital Structure

Capital structure refers to the proportion of owners' equity and long-term debt.

The generally followed norm of owners' equity and long-term debt in a company's capital structure is 50:50; owners' equity shall be 50%, and the long-term debt is 50%. It is only *indicative*. It can vary depending on the industry verticals.

Capital Gearing

Capital gearing is a technique for capital structure analysis and planning. Gearing means increasing the borrowing to increase owners' wealth. It involves decision-making on additional debt based on the after-tax cost of capital employed and after-tax return on investment.

Capital gearing varies based on the industry and within the industry over time. It is an advanced analytical model applied by finance professionals when deciding the company's capital structure.

∞

3. Long-term Debt

Long-term debt is usually in the form of term loans.

Banks lend term loans for a period ranging from three years to ten years. In exceptional cases, banks lend the term loans repayable in twenty years.

The loan period depends on the industry and the purpose of the borrowing. Repayment of term loans is by monthly or quarterly installments.

Some investments require time to generate the cash flow, from commissioning the plant to selling the products. To provide for this gap in cash generation, banks allow an initial holiday period for repayment, say up to nine months.

Remember, the **interest on the loan keeps accruing** during the repayment holiday period.

Banks lend long-term loans to finance a specific investment. In addition, the company should commit its share of funds for the investment.

Let's understand the term loan with an illustration.

Consider an investment of USD 100,000 for an additional production line. Following the norm for owners' equity and long-term debt at 50:50 as per the generally followed norm for capital structure, you make the term loan proposal for USD 50,000. The company contributes the remaining USD 50,000 from owners' equity.

4. What You Need to Get the Loan

You need to submit the loan proposal to the bank articulating the financial viability of the new investment.

Banks examine:

- ✓ If the borrower is financially sound,
- ✓ His proposal is economically viable,
- ✓ The borrower has a good record of accomplishment and
- ✓ There is security for the loan in the event of a default.

Thus, banks evaluate a loan application based on:

➢ Financial Strength
➢ Business Plan
➢ Financial Viability, and
➢ Collateral security

i) Financial Strength

a) Audited Financial Statements

Banks evaluate the financial strength by computing the company's net worth and financial ratios from the last three years' audited financial statements.

Net worth

Total assets minus total liabilities give the company's net worth. The net worth of a company reflects its financial strength.

Net worth computed for three years provides the banker whether the company is financially sound.

Financial Ratios

Debt-Equity Ratio: Lower the debt component in the capital employed than the industry average — higher is the ranking for additional lending.

$$\text{Debt-Equity Ratio} = \text{Long-term debt} / \text{Owners' Equity}$$

Alternate formula:

$$\text{Debt-Equity Ratio} = \text{Total debt} / \text{Owners' Equity}$$

Interest Coverage Ratio: Interest Coverage = Earnings before Interest and Taxes or EBIT / Interest Expense

Debt Service Coverage Ratio

$$\text{Debt Service Coverage} = \text{Net Operating Income} / \text{Annual Debt Services}$$

Where a) Net operating income = net profit + depreciation and amortization + interest expense, and

b) Debt services = principal + interest payments

Interest-coverage and debt-service-coverage ratios are key measures for the banks to determine if the cash flow would be sufficient to meet the repayment obligations.

b) Business Plan

From the above discussion, you may wonder how banks evaluate a new project.

For a new business proposal, banks critically analyze the *Business Plan*.

In this scenario, banks need a detailed business plan supported by

- ✓ Industrial & market survey from recognized institutions,
- ✓ Project cost estimate,
- ✓ Details of project funding by promoters, and
- ✓ Credit reference.

ii) Financial Viability

We need to convince the banker the project is financially viable. We prepare and submit *five-year financial projections* for the project.

How do we prepare a financial projection?

A Financial projection requires us to

a) Make realistic assumptions,

b) Prepare sales projections based on market research,

c) Prepare production plan based on projected sales, and

d) Compute cash flow projections based on sales and production projections.

Projected cash flow should cover both the principal and interest repayment and leave enough margins for the company's sustained growth.

iii) Collateral

Banks require *collateral to secure* their loans.

Collateral may include a mortgage of the company's assets, such as land & building and inventory. In addition, banks may require the personal guarantee of the promoters.

The above list of banks' requirements for lending is indicative only.

Actual requirements may differ based on the industry, individual banks approach, company's relationship and credit history with the bank, and the general economic outlook.

∞

5. EMI Mystery

Usually, the banks need the company to repay the term loans in Equated Monthly Installments.

In an EMI, the repayment amount remains the same for all loan installments. EMI make up two portions—i) interest and ii) principal. In the beginning, interest will be more, and the principal will be less. As the repayment progresses interest component reduces while the principal component increases.

Let us understand the EMI through a model.

Equated Monthly Installment (EMI) model				
Loan amount (Principal)				$10,000
No. of installments for repayment				4
Repayment terms				Monthly
Interest at flat rate				3.759%
Total amount of interest				$125
Interest rate on diminishing balance				6% per annum
Installment Month (a)	EMI (b)	Principal paid (c)	Interest paid (d)	Principal outstanding (e)
1	2,531.33	2,481.33	50.00	7,518.67
2	2,531.32	2,493.73	37.59	5,024.94
3	2,531.32	2,506.20	25.12	2,518.73
4	2,531.32	2,518.73	12.59	0.00
Total			125.30	

Exhibit 12.1

In the model, column (b) is what you pay monthly as installments. It remains unchanged (equal) throughout the loan period.

Column (c) gives the break-up, how much of your payment goes to repay the loan (principal amount). Column (d) shows how much you pay towards interest on the loan. The last column (d) provides how much your loan is outstanding after paying the installment.

Your bank will provide this information on a specific request, or your finance team can make the computation. You can Google for EMI calculator, and there are good websites, which provide EMI computed values.

The model in Exhibit 12.1 is made with four installments to make it the simplest. Here our objective is to understand the concept behind it. In practice, you will have installments of up to sixty months or even more.

Exhibit 12.2, we have one-hundred-twenty month installments, made simple by cutting a portion of it for presentation purposes.

EMI model with 120 months installment				
Loan amount (Principal)		$10,000,000		
No. of installments for repayment		120		
Repayment terms		Monthly		
Interest at flat rate		3.322%		
Total amount of interest		$3,322,460		
Rate of interest on diminishing balance		6% per annum		
Installment Month (a)	EMI (b)	Principal paid (c)	Interest paid (d)	Principal outstanding (e)
1	111,020.50	61,020.50	50,000.00	9,938,979.50
2	111,020.50	61,325.60	49,694.90	9,877,653.89
3	111,020.50	61,632.23	49,388.27	9,816,021.66
4	111,020.50	61,940.39	49,080.11	9,754,081.27
5	111,020.51	62,250.10	48,770.41	9,691,831.17
6	111,020.51	62,561.35	48,459.16	9,629,269.83
Rows 7th to 116 installments hidden...				
117	111,020.50	108,827.57	2,192.93	329,758.44
118	111,020.50	109,371.71	1,648.79	220,386.73
119	111,020.50	109,918.57	1,101.93	110,468.16
120	111,020.50	110,468.16	552.34	0.00
TOTAL			3,322,460.26	

Exhibit 12.2

Rate of Interest in an EMI Loan

While negotiating a loan with EMI payments, take care to understand the interest rate charged by the bank. Two types of interests are there in an EMI—i) *flat rate* and ii) *diminishing rate*.

i) Flat Rate of Interest

Under the flat rate, banks calculate interest on the original loan amount from the beginning to the end of the loan period without considering the repayments of the principal amount.

ii) Diminishing Rate

Banks calculate interest on the reduced outstanding loan amount during the repayment period.

For example, in the first installment, they calculate interest on the total loan amount. In the second installment, banks calculate interest on the original loan amount *less* the principal amount repaid in the first installment.

Don't get misled by the Flat Rate

The diminishing rate is the actual interest rate, and the flat rate of interest in an EMI is a misleading interest rate.

The flat rate would be considerably lower than the diminishing rate because it is made unrealistically low by applying it on the entire loan amount throughout the loan period.

Therefore, while negotiating a new loan with an EMI, consider *only the diminishing rate of interest* and not the flat rate of interest.

∞

6. Short Term Borrowing

Short-term loans are those borrowings with a maturity period of one year or less.

Companies use short-term borrowings to finance part of the working capital (page no.80.)

Examples:

- ✓ Cash-credit for inventory,
- ✓ Invoice discounting and factoring for Accounts Receivable,
- ✓ Overdraft for operating expenses.

Banks approve short-term loans with covenants (conditions.) The loan covenants may require the company to submit periodic stock statements, MIS reports and audited financial statements.

The covenants may also restrict the distribution of profits to the owners. Besides, banks require pledging of inventory, assignment of accounts receivables, and sometimes promoters' guarantee as security.

Usually, short-term loans are not subject to loan repayments. Short-term facilities are subject to renewal annually by the lending banks based on a credit appraisal.

i) Cash Credit

Cash credit is short-term lending by banks; loan amount is made available as per approved cash credit limit for financing a portion of the working capital, say the inventory.

ii) Overdraft

Overdraft (OD) is the most often used short-term credit facility from the banks.

Banks make available the OD facility through the company's regular operating bank account. The company can withdraw up to the overdraft loan limit.

There is no fixed repayment required for an overdraft loan facility. Such loans are revolving in nature. Some banks need the company to repay the entire loan amount for a certain number of days, say five days without a break once during the financial year.

Banks charge interest on the daily highest outstanding balance.

iii) Letter of Credit

LC facilities are used widely in present-day import and export transactions because it secures payment to the overseas seller and goods delivery to the buyer.

When the company imports goods, it approaches its bank to issue the LC, a payment guarantee favoring the overseas supplier for the value of goods.

The company should have a credit facility with the bank or deposit funds equivalent to the LC amount.

The buyer's bank issues the LC to the seller's bank. It is a guarantee to pay when the supplier submits the shipping documents.

Let's illustrate LC with an example.

1) Company A in India is importing machinery for USD 50,000 from Company B in the USA.
2) Company A has an LC facility with its bank for the import value.
3) Company A requests its banker to issue an LC to Company B's banker for USD 50,000; Bank issues the LC.
4) Company B completes the shipping and delivery and submits the documents to his bank requesting payment against the LC. His banker releases the amount to Co B and debits Co A's banker.
5) Co A's banker debits Co A's account. Additionally, the bank charges Co A its fee for the service.

Now the advantage is obvious: The importer and the exporter have to complete their trade obligations.

iv) Invoice Discounting

Invoice discounting is borrowing against credit sales. The bank lends a portion of the customer invoice amount to the company during the credit period.

The borrowing company submits copies of the customer invoices and borrows loans up to the discount percentage on the value of the submitted invoice.

The discount percentage is as per the company's loan agreement with the bank. It may vary between seventy-five to eighty percent.

The customer pays against the invoice on the due date; the company deposits the customer's check to a trust account controlled by the bank.

Bank releases the difference between the invoice amount and the discount percentage lent already deducting his fee for the service.

Let's understand invoice discounting with an example:

1) Your company sells goods for USD10,000 with two months credit periods.
2) Consider the company has a discounting arrangement with the bank at a discount percentage of 80%. Bank's fee for the service is 3%.
3) The company now discounts the sales invoice USD 10,000 with the bank and gets a loan of USD 8,000 immediately.
4) After two months, the customer pays USD 10,000 by check, and the company deposits the check into the trust account controlled by the bank.
5) Bank deducts USD 8,000, amount lent on the customer invoice.
6) Bank also deducts USD 240 (3% of USD 8,000) and credits the balance amount of USD 1,760 to the company's bank account.

Word of Caution: Invoice discounting comes at a higher cost compared to other forms of bank borrowings. Therefore, it is not the preferred means of borrowing.

∞

Chapter Recap

Gain knowledge of your company's capital structure — the proportion of debt and equity to know how it influences the borrowing capacity.

While deciding a loan option, know the actual interest rate on a long-term loan in an EMI as given by the diminishing interest rate.

Understand banks' requirements to grant a loan; it helps you do your homework beforehand and approach the bank from a position of strength.

∞∞

Author's Endnote

I trust this book helps you in a small way for your enormous success as an entrepreneur or corporate executive. I wish you the very best in your professional life.

∞∞∞

Thank You for Reading

I have tried to make the subject as simple as possible while covering all topics and necessary jargon you need in finance.

Have you found this book helpful? Has it delivered what it promised? In case if you are not satisfied, be kind to send me a note at murugesan0202@yahoo.com.

If you have enjoyed reading this book and feel benefited, please leave your honest review and ratings.

As an author, I read every review, and it helps me improve this book.

You may leave your review on the amazon page:

USA	http://bit.ly/finance475
India	http://bit.ly/finance485
UK	http://bit.ly/finance495
France	http://bit.ly/finance465

Your few words of appreciation mean so much to me!

Your pal,

Murugesan Ramaswamy

∞∞∞

Other Title by the Author

SAP FICO Beginner's Handbook

Explaining SAP **FI, CO Modules & Concepts** to guide Consultants, Users, End Users gain confidence, get comfortable with, and improve productivity using SAP FICO. To know more about the book: https://sapficouser.com/home/sapficobooks/

∞∞

Connect with the Author

You can contact the author at: murugesan0202@yahoo.com, admin@sapficouser.com

For updates on new releases & subscribing to SAP FICO USER News Letter, please visit: https://sapficouser.com

THANK YOU FOR YOUR SUPPORT!

∞∞∞

Related Resource

If you are from India and haven't explored investing in Mutual Funds like me, I would suggest an eBook, which I found helpful. This book gives a quick overview of how to benefit from investing in Mutual Funds:

Title: **The Exciting World of Indian Mutual Funds**

Authored by **Madhusudan Sohani**

Available at Amazon.in: http://amzn.to/2BgtOms

Amazon.in Ref **ASIN: B078XKDWWM**

∞∞∞∞